S0-AFS-152

PROFESSOR MURPHY'S
POSITIVELY
PERPLEXING
GAMES
&
TRICKS

This edition published by Parragon Books Ltd in 2015 and distributed by

Parragon Inc.
440 Park Avenue South, 13th Floor
New York, NY 10016
www.parragon.com

Copyright © Parragon Books Ltd 2015

Produced by Tall Tree Books

All rights reserved. No part of this publication may be reproduced, stored in a retrieval system, or transmitted, in any form or by any means, electronic, mechanical, photocopying, recording, or otherwise, without the prior permission of the copyright holder.

ISBN 978-1-4723-7657-2

Printed in China

PROFESSOR MURPHY'S

POSITIVELY PERPLEXING

GAMES

&

TRICKS

PaRragon

Bath · New York · Cologne · Melbourne · Delhi
Hong Kong · Shenzhen · Singapore · Amsterdam

CONTENTS

	page
Introduction	6
1. TRA (ART BACKWARD)	8
2. SNAP!	9
3. CHARADES	10
4. SARDINES	12
5. WINK MURDER	13
6. WORDS AND PICTURES	14
7. ELEPHANT	15
8. THE LOST CARD	16
9. CHATTERBOX	18
10. FENCE ME IN	19
11. CAVE-DWELLER BOULDERS	20
12. IT'S BEHIND YOU!	21
13. WORD BUILDER	22
14. KIM'S GAME	23
15. DISAPPEARING MONEY	24
16. PICK-UP STICKS	26
17. DOODLE MONSTER	27
18. FLAPPY FISH RACING	28
19. THE INTERROGATOR	29
20. KETCHUP MIND CONTROL	30
21. SLAP-CLAP-SNAP!	32
22. PANTS ON FIRE	33
23. PAIRS	34
24. BEETLE	35
25. CUTTING THE LADY IN HALF	36
26. STRETCH-A-SKETCH	38

	page
27. HANGMAN	39
28. BLACKJACK	40
29. BUZZ	41
30. GET KNOTTED!	42
31. TIC-TAC-TOE	43
32. BATTLESHIPS	44
33. PICTURE THIS	46
34. STRING RELAY	47
35. VANISHING COTTON SWAB	48
36. WORD RACE	50
37. CAR CODES	51
38. LORD OF THE RING	52
39. TWENTY QUESTIONS	53
40. DISSOLVING COIN	54
41. BLINDMAN'S BLUFF	56
42. CENTURY	57
43. MILLENNIUM	58
44. WHO'S AT THE PARTY?	59
45. CATCH THE QUEEN	60
46. THREE-IN-A-ROW	61
47. WORD LADDERS	62
48. THE MAGIC STRAW	63
49. CLIP THE CLIPS	64
50. ALPHABET MARKET	65
51. JUMPING RUBBER BAND	66
52. BOXES	67
53. LEG LISTS	69

	page		page
54. THE FLOATING CARD	70	80. TUMBLING EGGS	102
55. IMPOSSIBLE PAPER	72	81. DOWSING FOR CARDS	103
56. HOT AND COLD	73	82. TIP-TAP HANDS	104
57. INDESTRUCTIBLE STRING	74	83. CONSEQUENCES	105
58. MURDER IN THE DARK	76	84. BINGO	106
59. CRAZY EIGHTS	77	85. CROSSWORDS	107
60. SELF-SLICING BANANA	78	86. WISH YOU WERE HERE	108
61. WORD LINKS	79	87. SNAKE TRAP	110
62. MONEY MATTERS	80	88. BLOW FOOTBALL	111
63. PIN THE TAIL ON THE DONKEY	81	89. IT'S IN THE CARDS	112
		90. RHYME TIME	113
64. THE CLIMBING RING	82	91. ACROSTICS	114
65. FLYING PENCIL	84	92. NUMBER MAGIC	115
66. MIND READING	85	93. SECRET FOURS	116
67. BOTTLE UP	86	94. TABOO	117
68. ART GALLERY	87	95. SHROUD OF MYSTERY	118
69. THE FORTUNE-TELLER	88	96. REVERSE CARD	120
70. FLOATING PENCIL	90	97. IT BEGINS WITH . . .	121
71. ANAGRAMS	91	98. MIXED MESSAGES	122
72. TREASURE HUNT	92	99. FIND THE COIN	123
73. FISHING FOR ICE CUBES	93	100. MINI WORDS	124
74. THE SECRET COIN	94	101. GIN RUMMY	125
75. CHEAT	96	102. ALPHA RACE	126
76. FIFTEENS	97	103. THE NAME GAME	127
77. THE TOOTHPICK TRICK	98	104. COMBINATION CODES	128
78. STANDING TUBE	100		
79. LIMERICK TAG	101		

INTRODUCTION

When it comes to having fun with friends and family, nothing beats playing a few games to get people talking, laughing, and relaxing together. There is, of course, always an element of competition involved in playing games, and that helps to make playing them together all the more enjoyable—for grown-ups as well as children.

Party games are hugely entertaining, but party tricks provide a completely different kind of entertainment. Conjuring tricks, illusions, sleight of hand, and card tricks can amaze and enthrall an audience, and you're never too young or too old to learn new tricks.

Everything in this book is designed for everyone to enjoy together, whether at a family gathering, a birthday party, or simply when trying to brighten up a rainy day. I'm sure you are going to have as much fun playing and performing as I did putting together this whole selection of games and tricks!

Prof WP Murphy

Professor's tip:
Never focus solely on winning when you are playing a game. Enjoy yourself while taking part, and you will always be a winner!

Included in the Professor's compendium of games is a selection of tried-and-true, traditional family pastimes that have been keeping children, parents, and grandparents amused for many years. There are also some that have been given a modern twist to keep younger participants interested and to keep older players on their toes!

Tricks can require some preparation but most involve using only items that can generally be found around the house.

For young children, games and tricks marked with this symbol will require adult assistance or supervision due to the inclusion of sharp or small objects or the use of glue.

TRA (ART Backward)

The object of this game is really simple. All you have to do is to draw a picture of something suggested by one of the other players—a house, a cow, a car, or a flower, perhaps —but you must not look at the paper. You can do your drawing only by looking in a mirror.

What you will need:

• A mirror • A pen or pencil
• Paper for drawing on • A book or magazine to lean on

What you must do:

Each player must take a turn at creating a drawing. If you have a small mirror that can stand on a table or be propped up against a wall, that is ideal. Lay your sheet of paper down so that you can see it in the mirror, and then draw your picture without looking directly at the paper—it's a lot harder than it sounds! If you have a large wall mirror, use it to play the game, by getting each player to take turns standing in front of the mirror holding the drawing paper against their body. You will need to use a book or magazine under the paper to play the game this way.

The results are usually hilarious and will probably be the worst, shakiest, and most scribbly sketches you have ever done, so don't be upset if everyone else laughs at your drawings. The whole point of this game is for everyone to have some fun.
Once everyone has had a turn, you can vote for the funniest drawing and the most hopelessly backward TSITRA!

Professor's tip:
Backward drawing is not easy, but if you concentrate hard, you can soon get the hang of it.

SNAP!

2+ PLAYERS

This is an easy card game, but you have to keep your wits about you because it can move very fast. You can play with more than eight players, but it then becomes a little too spread out, and it can be difficult to see exactly what is happening.

What you will need:

• A pack of cards

What you must do:

All of the players sit around a table and the dealer deals the cards face down, one to each player, until all the cards have been dealt. The cards remain face down, but players must sort their own into a neat stack.

The player to the left of the dealer starts. He takes the top card from his stack and places it down face up so that everyone can see it, starting a new stack. The next player then takes the top card from his stack and places it down to start his own face-up stack. Everyone must do the same, taking turns, watching as a new card is turned over.

If a player turns over a new card that matches the top card on any other player's face-up stack, the first player to shout "Snap!" wins all of the cards from the face-up stacks of the one who has just played, and the one who has the matching card. The dealer decides who was first to shout. Matching cards have to be of the same type—a two of hearts matches a two of spades, clubs, or diamonds; a queen of clubs matches a queen of hearts, diamonds, or spades.

The game continues until one player has won all of the cards. If you run out of cards to turn over but still have some in your face-up stack, you stay in the game waiting to spot a "Snap!" and win some cards to continue.

9

CHARADES

4+ PLAYERS

Charades is a great game that can be played by large groups that include players of all ages. It gives everyone a chance to show off their acting skills, although the acting has to be mimed because the player is not allowed to speak.

What you must do:

If you are the first player to take a turn, you must think of the title of a book, movie, play, TV show, or song. You then have to stand in front of all of the others and mime clues for them to guess the title.

To begin with, the player has to let everyone know in which category their chosen title belongs. For this part, there are accepted mimes.

For a book, press your hands together, palms inward, and then open them up as though you are opening a book.

For a movie, hold your left fist up to your eye (some use the nose) as though you have a movie camera in front of your face, and circle your right fist in the air at the side as though you are turning the crank on an ancient movie camera.

For a play, hold your arms together in front of you, and then sweep them up to the sides as though they are stage curtains.

For a TV show, hold your two forefingers together in front of you, then move them apart, down, and back together to trace the shape of a TV screen in the air.

For a song, hold your mouth open and throw your hands out from your chest like an opera singer.

The others will shout out "Movie!" if it's a movie, and you point to the first one to shout and put your other index finger on your nose to indicate that they are correct.

Now you have to hold up the number of fingers that corresponds to the number of words in your title. If your title is *The Empire Strikes Back*, then hold up four fingers to indicate four words. Someone will call out "Four words!" and you point and touch your nose to show they are correct. We can use this title to demonstrate some of the mime techniques you are allowed to use. Remember that you are not allowed to speak, mouth words, or make noises, but you can point at objects in the room if that helps.

The others will shout out guesses during your mime, so it is important that you point to someone who guesses part of your title correctly and touch your nose. That way, everyone knows how the guessing is going.

There are some accepted ways of miming certain words. If it is a small word, like "the," you hold your thumb and forefinger close together to show everyone a small space. People will guess "But," "An," or "It," but someone will eventually say "the." Point and touch your nose.

"Empire" is a tricky word to mime, so hold up three fingers to show that you are going for the third word. You can then mime hitting something, or even swinging a baseball bat for "strike." People will shout "club," "hit," and so on, but someone will get "strike." Point and touch your nose, then use your sign for a small word but widen the gap to show that the word you are looking for is bigger than "strike" and they will guess "strikes."

Hold up four fingers to show you are doing the fourth word. Point to your back. Once they've guessed "back," they will be pondering over "The (something) Strikes Back …"

Hold up two fingers to show you are doing the second word. Tap the two fingers on your forearm to show that the word has two syllables (em-pire). Hold up two fingers again, and place them on your forearm to show you are giving them the second syllable. Give your earlobe a tug. This is the sign for "sounds like," and you can use it for a syllable, a whole word or an entire title. You could try miming warming your hands by a fire, which sounds a little like "pire," and from that, your audience would have "The Fire Strikes Back." Surely they would then guess the title?

The person who guesses first is the next person to mime a title in front of everyone, and you can now relax and take part in the guessing.

Professor's tip:
If you think that you can act out an entire title rather than doing individual words, draw a big circle in the air to show everyone you are doing the whole thing, and go for it!

11

4

3+ PLAYERS

SARDINES

This game is hide-and-seek with a difference; the main difference is that everyone, except the first person to hide, is a seeker, and everyone, except the last seeker, is a hider!

What you will need:

• A clock or watch

What you must do:

All the players gather in one room, and one is chosen to go and hide somewhere else in the house. While the first player is gone, the others must decide, using the alphabetical order of their names or whatever other method they choose, who will go next.

The second player leaves the room one minute after the first player and must seek out the first player. The first player will have hidden behind a sofa in the corner of a room, in a closet, under a bed—somewhere suitably concealing. When player 2 finds player 1, they must squeeze into the hiding place together without making a sound because player 3 will soon be hunting for them. When player 3 finds them, all three must squeeze in together, and so it continues until all the players are packed in like sardines in a can.

It can happen that player 3 bumps into player 2 while player 2 is still seeking out player 1. They can choose to work together, but they must stay silent. Outside of the main room, there is no talking.

Once everyone has squeezed in together, you can go back to the main room and start again.

5 WINK MURDER

5+ PLAYERS

An easily portable game, you can play Wink Murder in your living room, on a picnic, or anywhere that you can gather enough people together around a table or sitting in a circle.

What you will need:

• A pack of cards

What you must do:

You have to count out as many cards as there are players. These can be any cards but must include the ace of spades and the ace of hearts. The players look at their cards but must not show anyone else.

The player who gets the ace of hearts is the detective and must tell everyone. The player who gets the ace of spades is the murderer and, like all of the other players, stays silent. The players now talk to each other while the detective tries to discover who the murderer is by seeing him or her winking.

The murderer has to blend in with the other players, but when he or she catches a player's eye and winks, that player has been murdered and can make a big show of dying with shrieks, groans, and a lot of flopping around. Basically, if you are killed, die as dramatically as possible!

The detective has to spot the murderer before all the other players become victims, and obviously, nobody else is allowed to wink. Once the murderer is caught, or only the detective and the murderer are left, you can start all over again.

13

6

2+
PLAYERS

WORDS AND PICTURES

Use your imagination to create bizarre pictures and captions.

What you will need:

• A sheet of paper for everyone • A pencil for everyone

What you must do:

The whole point of this game is to create the silliest pictures and captions that you can dream up, so that everyone can laugh at the end result.

Everyone starts with a sheet of paper. At the top, write a caption like, "The dog's tail wagged around and around when it saw its food bowl."

Everyone then passes their paper to the person sitting on their right. Now you all have a paper with someone else's caption at the top. Your task now is to draw a picture beneath the caption, showing what you think is going on in the caption.

Next, fold the paper over at the top to hide the caption, and pass the paper to your right. Everyone now has a drawing in front of them. Add a caption below it. The player with the dog and bowl might think it is "Helicopter hound meets alien ship."

The top of the paper must now be folded over again, so that the drawing is now hidden and the paper passed on to the right with only the new caption showing. This time, everyone must draw something to go with that caption.

Keep going like that—writing, drawing, writing, drawing—until the paper is full. Then you can unfold the paper in front of you and read out the strangest illustrated story ever, holding it up so that everyone can see the weird drawings. There are no winners and losers—it's all just to make each other laugh!

14

7

2+ PLAYERS

ELEPHANT

The last one to turn into an elephant is the loser!

What you will need:

• A pack of cards • A piece of paper • A pencil

What you must do:

Select a set of four cards for each player—four eights, four queens and so forth—then put all of the other cards aside.

The dealer now draws an elephant and puts it in the middle of the table. He or she then shuffles the selected cards and deals each player four.

The players look at their cards. The aim is to end up with four matching cards. If no one immediately has a set of four, then the dealer calls "Pass," and everyone takes one card from their hand and passes it to their left.

This continues until someone gets a set of four. If you do, you say nothing: You just put your thumb on your nose with your little finger pointing outward to make an elephant's trunk. Quick as they can, everyone does the same, and the last to make a trunk takes the elephant from the middle. They keep the elephant until the next round when someone else may win it by being last.

15

THE LOST CARD

2+
PLAYERS

Amaze your friends when you have them "lose" a card that they have chosen from a deck, and you find it without having known what the card was.

What you will need:

• A deck of cards

What you must do:

A little preparation is required for this trick, and it has to be done before you present the trick so that no one sees you doing it. You have to remove all of the spades from the deck and put them in order, counting the ace as "1" and the king as "13." Return the spades to the deck at the bottom with the ace at the very bottom. Your deck of cards, standing face down, will now have the ace of spades facing the table, and above it will be 2, 3, 4, 5, up to king of spades, with the rest of the pack stacked above the king.

Hold the deck out toward a willing volunteer, and ask him or her to choose a card. You have to make sure that they do not disturb the bottom 13 cards in the deck, so grip the deck near the bottom with your thumb and forefinger to protect the spades you have put there.

Your volunteer can look at the card but must not show you. Ask the volunteer to cut the deck, taking half the deck off the top and setting it aside face down. The volunteer must then put the chosen card on top of the pile set aside and place the other pile on top. The chosen card is now hidden in the middle of the deck, but because you know that the ace to king of spades were originally on the bottom of the deck, the ace is now sitting on top of the chosen card.

The volunteer now has to turn the deck face up and cut the deck, which will reveal a new card on top of the remaining pile. If this card is not a spade, tell the volunteer to complete the cut by placing the remaining pile on top of the new pile, still face up. They must then cut again until a spade is revealed. Do not let your volunteer know that you are looking for a spade.

16

If the spade that is revealed is, for instance, the five, it means that the four, three, two, ace, and then the chosen card are now on the bottom of the pile just set aside. The volunteer can complete the cut, then ask him or her to turn the deck over so that the cards are now face down.

You know that the top card on the deck is now the four of spades. Ask your volunteer to start taking cards from the top of the deck one at a time without turning them over. Without seeing what they are, he or she will take the four of spades, then the three, then the two, then the ace, then the chosen card. Stop the volunteer, ask him or her to turn over that card, and then say, "This is the card that you chose!"

Obviously, at the stage when the deck is being cut face up, if the nine of spades appears, the chosen card will end up as the ninth from the top; if it is the jack of spades, it will be the eleventh, and so on.

1. If the king of diamonds is chosen, you will not be shown it and it will be placed face down on top of the right-hand side of the cut deck.

2. The deck is turned over for the face-up cuts. Each cut must be completed and a new one started until a spade appears.

3. If a five of spades has appeared, you know that the king will be the fifth card from the top of the pile when the deck is turned over again.

Professor's tip:
Be sure to let your volunteer do all of the cutting, so that you do not have to touch the cards, and the trick will seem even more amazing.

9

Chatterbox

2+ PLAYERS

Anyone who loves to chatter about nothing in particular will become a grand champion at this game in just 30 seconds!

What you will need:

• A watch or clock • A piece of paper and a pencil for each player (or at least enough pencils to share) • A bowl, hat, or bag

What you must do:

Each player writes a topic on a piece of paper, and the papers are all put into the bowl or hat. The first player then picks out a topic. The object of the game is to talk about the topic for 30 seconds nonstop without repeating words (you can repeat words like "the" or "and" but not words that are important to the topic), without stumbling over your words or pausing, and without talking about things that have nothing to do with the topic.

The players must all choose the umpire, who will be in charge of timing, and decide if there has been repetition or any other rule-breaking by the speaker. The other players can shout "object" if they think there has been a pause, repeated words or the speaker has gone off the topic, but the umpire makes the final decision. The umpire will stop the clock while the objection is discussed, and he or she must decide whether to accept it or overrule it.

If accepted, the player who made the objection must take over the topic, speaking for whatever time is left. If rejected, the original player takes up the story again and must try to keep talking until the 30 seconds are up.

The umpire can award points to players for successful objections or successfully completed topics. Once the first topic is exhausted, a new player chooses a paper from the hat.

Professor's tip:
When you are talking, don't get yourself confused by trying to talk about history or technical things. Stick to your own opinions on the topic to avoid getting flustered!

18

FENCE ME IN

No ordinary connect-the-dots challenge. You'll have to think fast to win this game.

What you will need:

• A large sheet of paper • A pencil

What you must do:

Mark out a grid of dots on the paper. A grid that is ten dots by ten dots should make for a good game. The players each take turns to draw one horizontal or vertical line on the grid connecting two dots that are side by side. If the line that you draw closes off fences in a square, write your initials in the square and take another turn.

Once there are lots of lines on the grid, it may be that one player is able to fence in a square, take another turn, fence in another square, and keep going several times.

The player with most squares when the grid is full is the winner.

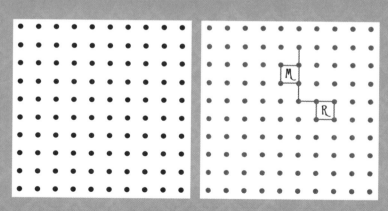

19

CAVE-DWELLER BOULDERS

2+ PLAYERS

You need space to create a bowling alley for this game, and you'll have to build a cave to bowl your boulders into.

What you will need:

• A cardboard box—a shoe box is ideal, but almost any cardboard box will do • A pair of scissors • A pen • Some marbles

What you must do:

The first thing to do is create your cave. Take the lid off the cardboard box or cut off the top. It needs to be turned upside down on the floor, so that it can sit with its "walls" directly on the floor. You now have to cut a series of entrances to your cave. These doors can be arches, or triangles, or thin slots. When your cave is on the ground, you will be trying to get marbles (your boulders) in through these openings.

Use the pen to mark a score above the openings. If it is a narrow opening, give it a high score of ten. If it is a wide opening and easier to aim for, give it a low score of two or three.

Each player, or cave dweller, then takes turns to roll a boulder at the cave. You win points for getting your boulder inside. If you miss and your boulder is sitting outside the cave, or you score and it rolls back out, you must leave it there. Another cave dweller may knock it in and can claim the points. The one with most points when everyone has used all their boulders is the winner.

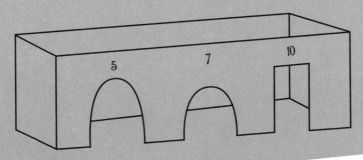

12

4+ PLAYERS

IT'S BEHIND YOU!

Be the first to find out what animal is sneaking up behind your back!

What you will need:

• Paper and pencils for all players • Tape

What you must do:

Each player has to draw an animal, a bird, or a fish on their piece of paper. It's probably a good idea to write the name of the animal as well, just in case the drawing isn't too recognizable.

The players must not let any other players see what they are drawing. The drawings are all then handed to a referee who keeps them safe while all of the players line up. The referee then uses the tape to attach a drawing, at random, to the back of each player.

The players can't see what animal is behind them, and they must all stand in a circle facing each other. Players take turns to turn around, show everyone their animal, turn back, and ask one question, such as "Does it have feathers?" or "Can you ride on its back?" The other players must answer truthfully but can only call out yes or no.

When one player's question has been answered, the next player shows their animal. When a player has asked enough questions to guess what animal is sneaking up behind him, on his next turn he can ask the question, "Is it an eagle?" or "Is it a camel?" If he's right, he sits down, and the rest continue until everyone has guessed correctly.

Word Builder

You can improve your spelling and vocabulary with this game, but the aim is never to finish writing a word.

What you will need:

• Paper and pencil • A dictionary

What you must do:

The first player writes a letter on the piece of paper. The next player adds a letter that could go toward building a word, and each player takes turns adding a letter, always making sure that the letter they add could be the next part of a word. If challenged, they have to say the word that they think could be made. Ultimately, one player will have to add a letter that completes the word, and that player loses a "life." Lose six lives and you're out of the game.

For example, if four players were playing:

Player 1 writes	P	
Player 2 writes	R	This could make "prove" or "pray," etc
Player 3 writes	A	"Pray" is still a possibility, or "prairie"
Player 4 writes	C	Now we could have "practice"
Player 1 writes	T	"Practice" looks like it might end up as the word
Player 2 writes	I	"Practice" is still on
Player 3 writes	C	"Practice" would mean Player 4 loses a life
Player 4 writes	A	Player 4 has saved a life by aiming for "practical"
Player 1 writes	L	Player 1 loses a life

Player 1 could have written B instead of L, aiming for "practicable," but would have to have known that word.

Three-letter words make the game too short. Words like "the" or "and" can be expanded to make "theory" or "android;" and so you should never end on a three-letter word, but do keep a dictionary handy to settle any disputes!

KIM'S GAME

When the character Kim was being trained as a spy in Rudyard Kipling's 1901 novel *Kim*, this game was used to improve his ability to remember lots of details.

What you will need:

• A tray • A cloth big enough to cover the tray • 15 to 20 objects
• A clock or watch • Paper and pencils for each player

What you must do:

This game needs a Memory Master who must be in charge and set up the game.

The Memory Master has to arrange at least 15, but not more than 20, objects on a tray and write down what each one is. The Memory Master then covers the objects with the cloth and places the tray in the middle of a table where everyone can see it.

The Memory Master uncovers the objects, giving everyone exactly one minute to study the tray and remember what is there. When time is up, the tray is covered again, and the players have two minutes to write down as many of the objects as they can remember.

Players get a point for every object they remember but lose a point if they list something that was not actually there.

Then, while everyone turns away, the Memory Master removes one item from the tray and calls for everyone to turn around again. The first player to spot what is missing gets five points.

The one with the most points is the winner.

Professor's tip:
It can help to try to remember objects in patterns on the tray, such as "the four in a square top right" or "the three in a triangle bottom left."

15

DISAPPEARING MONEY

2+
PLAYERS

There's a twist to this magic trick in that your money doesn't want to disappear and stays right where you left it!

What you will need:

- A light cloth such as a dish towel
- An orange (or an apple) • A coin

What you must do:

Tell your audience that you are going to make a coin disappear off the table in front of you, but try to appear a little uncertain about the trick, and let them know that you have had problems with it before—this is all part of your act.

Place the coin on the table in front of you, and slide it around a little as you are talking to your audience. Tell them that you are going to cover the coin with the cloth, but admit that they then won't be able to see where the coin is. You are sliding the coin to let them get used to the sound of the coin on the table—but don't tell them that.

So that they can see where the coin is at all times, place the orange on top of the coin. Now cover both with the cloth, and pinch the cloth in around the bottom of the orange by making a frame with your forefingers and thumbs.

Move the cloth around on the table, and the audience will hear that the coin is still there. Ask them to concentrate hard on helping you to make the coin disappear, and move the cloth toward you, away from you and from side to side. They can still hear the coin, so obviously the trick hasn't worked yet.

Try again, pulling the cloth toward you with your hands always maintaining the frame around the orange. Everyone can still hear the coin.

Now you must appear to lose your temper a little and quickly whack the cloth-covered orange with your hand. It flattens. You remove the cloth, and the coin is still there—but the orange has disappeared!

The trick is to move your thumbs apart for a moment when you pull the cloth towards you the last time. You have to let the orange roll off the coin, off the edge of the table and into your lap, all under the cover of the cloth. By keeping your forefingers in place, you can keep the round, orange-shaped bulge in the cloth, so everyone thinks the orange is still there. They can hear the coin, after all, so they think that both are still under the cloth when you flatten it.

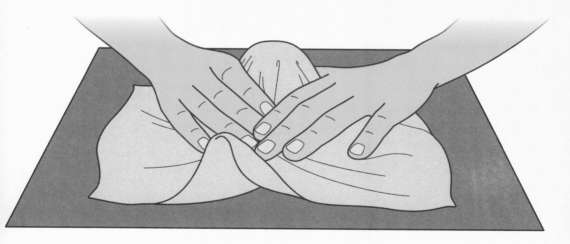

Gather the cloth around the orange, and support it so that it will keep its shape when you secretly drop the orange into your lap.

Professor's tip:
Practice makes perfect. Practice moving the orange around under the cloth, and practice dropping it into your lap, talking all the time to distract your audience.

PICK-UP STICKS

This is a race with a difference because you are aiming to be last!

What you will need:

• As many toothpicks as you can lay your hands on (at least 25)

What you must do:

Lay out the toothpicks neatly in columns and rows, so that they all line up like soldiers on a parade ground. You should try to have as many columns as you do rows, so if you lay out a first row of five toothpicks, you will need another four rows beneath it. You can have ten or more columns and rows, depending on how many toothpicks you have, but you should have at least five (diagram 1).

The players take turns picking up toothpicks. You can pick up as many as you like from a column or row, as long as they are next to each other with no gaps created by missing toothpicks that have already been picked up.

The first player might pick up the entire second row, for instance (diagram 2). The second player can then pick up all of rows 1, 3, or 4 but only either the first toothpick in one of the columns or from the third toothpick to the end of any column.

The aim, remember, is to be last to pick up, so thinking ahead and leaving gaps that stop your opponent from picking up everything that remains is the key to winning.

Diagram 1

Diagram 2

DOODLE MONSTER

Use your creative talents to turn a scribble into a creature as fabulous as your imagination can conjure up.

What you will need:

- Colored pencils
- Paper • A watch or clock

What you must do:

Each of the players sitting around a table draws a squiggle on a piece of paper and passes it on to the player sitting to the right.

The players then have ten minutes to turn the squiggle into the most fantastic monster that they can think of. It can be part animal, part robot, or lots of parts of different animals—anything goes.

After ten minutes, the players can all have a good laugh at each other's drawings as they explain, one by one, what their creature is, where it lives, and what it eats. They can then vote for the scariest, weirdest, and funniest efforts.

Flappy Fish Racing

 3+ PLAYERS

Flappy Fish Racing is a lot of fun, but if you aren't crazy about fish, then don't worry. Real fish are not required, but you do need real jockeys. Each player is a fish jockey, racing his or her own fish. If you are in charge, you must be the starter and also decide who has won at the end of the race.

What you will need:

• An old newspaper • A pair of scissors
• A marker • A selection of magazines

What you must do:

Use the marker to draw a fish shape on the newspaper. Make it nice and fat and at least 1 foot long.

Cut out the fish, but cut through several layers of the newspaper at once, so that you have several identical fish.

Each of the jockeys then writes his or her name on a fish.

Lay the fish flat on the floor along a starting line, with their heads pointing toward a finish line on the other side of the room.

Each jockey is given a magazine and put under starter's orders.

The starter calls "Paddle!" and the jockeys flap their magazines, slapping them on the floor to make a draft and blow their fish toward the finish line.

The fish may get mixed up when they flap off in all directions, but the first to cross the line wins, no matter which jockey gave it the final flap.

Professor's tip:
You will need lots of floor space for Flappy Fish Racing, but it can get a bit crowded with too many jockeys. Run separate, smaller races; then the winners can compete in a grand final.

THE INTERROGATOR

3+ PLAYERS

The whole point of this game is to answer The Interrogator's questions without cracking a smile—but keeping a straight face is not as easy as you might think. Usually, you have to think of an answer when you are asked a question, but in this game, you already know the answer—it's the question that takes you by surprise!

At the start of the game, all of the players have to agree on a phrase that will be the answer to The Interrogator's questions, no matter what the questions are. The sillier you make the phrase, the better, and everyone must answer the questions using the same phrase. Let's say you make the phrase "A kangaroo wearing a pirate's hat."

One player must now take the first turn at being The Interrogator. His or her job is to make you smile or giggle when you give your answer, and The Interrogator can ask anything at all. The Interrogator's first question might be, "What did you have for breakfast?" You must answer, "A kangaroo wearing a pirate's hat."

If you answer without smiling or giggling, then The Interrogator moves on to the next player and makes up another question, such as, "What does your math teacher look like?" or "Who goes to work on a unicycle?" or "What do you see when you look in a mirror?"

Smile or giggle and you're out, but you then become the new Interrogator, and you can decide what the new answer phrase is.

20

KETCHUP MIND CONTROL

3+ PLAYERS

We all love ketchup, right? Well, almost all of us—but nobody likes messing around with those clumsy little packets. Even if you can find the easy way to open one, you know you're going to end up with ketchup dribbling between your fingers or splashing on your shirt. So how much more would you love ketchup if you could control one of those packets using only the power of your mind?

That's the kind of introduction that you need to give your audience before you go on to amaze them by demonstrating ketchup mind control. You will make an intact, unopened packet of ketchup rise, fall, and even hover inside a sealed plastic bottle full of water. There's no way you can physically touch it, yet you will be able to make it move.

What you will need:

- One large, clear plastic bottle with a screw top and any labels removed, so that you can see straight through it
- One unopened packet of ketchup

What you must do:

Fill the bottle with water, and fold or scrunch the packet a little in order to push it lengthwise into the bottle, so that it sits in the water the right way up. A little water will be displaced and spill out, but don't worry about that.

Screw the lid back on the bottle. The ketchup will be floating near the top of the bottle. Talk to your audience, tell them what you are doing, and encourage them to concentrate on the ketchup.

Now grip the bottle in one hand, with your fingers toward the audience and your thumb on your side of the bottle. Your fingers will obviously hide part of the bottle, but everyone will still be able to see the ketchup moving at your command.

Next, use your free hand to wave at the ketchup and call out "Down! Down! Down!" Make sure that everyone else is concentrating and joining in. The trick is then secretly to squeeze the bottle slightly, without letting the audience see you do it. A gentle squeeze will make the ketchup packet sink to the bottom.

Command the packet to "Rise! Rise! Rise!" and relax your squeezing hand, again without letting the audience see you doing it. The packet will float upward inside the bottle. With a little practice, you should be able to judge your squeeze so that you can make the ketchup "hover" halfway up the bottle, but remember to grip the bottle with your fingers toward the audience. If you hold the bottle to one side, they will be able to see your secret squeeze. Always remember to keep talking and make lots of movements with your free hand to disguise the fact that you are squeezing the bottle.

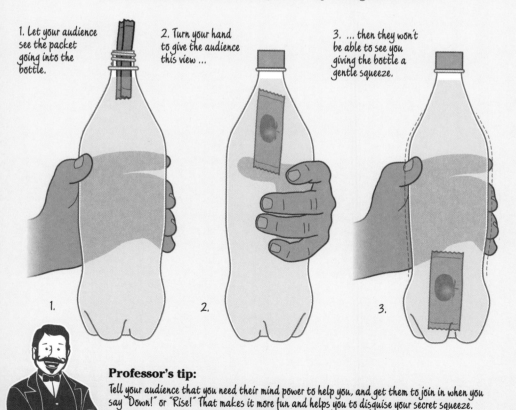

1. Let your audience see the packet going into the bottle.

2. Turn your hand to give the audience this view ...

3. ... then they won't be able to see you giving the bottle a gentle squeeze.

1.

2.

3.

Professor's tip:

Tell your audience that you need their mind power to help you, and get them to join in when you say "Down!" or "Rise!" That makes it more fun and helps you to disguise your secret squeeze.

SLAP-CLAP-SNAP!

3+ PLAYERS

This game is all about being able to concentrate, keep to a rhythm, and think quickly. Once the game is underway, a little distraction or someone getting the giggles can be enough for you to lose the beat and crash out of the game.

What you must do:

The idea is simple. Once everyone is sitting in a circle, you get the rhythm going. Everyone slaps both hands on their knees, claps, and then snaps their fingers left and right. This sets up the beat—slap, clap, snap, snap—1, 2, 3, 4.

The person who starts the game must have a topic in mind. If the topic is, for example, famous movies, then he or she chants, "Names-of, fam-ous, mov-ies." The chanting comes on the slap-clap beats: "Names(slap)–of (clap)," with the snap-snap giving two beats pause before "Fam(slap)–ous(clap)," and another snap-snap before "Mov(slap)–ies(clap)."

That gets you going. After "Mov-ies" there is a snap-snap pause before the next player in the circle gives a movie name, again on the slap-clap beat. It could be "*Star*(slap)–*Wars*(clap)." There is then a snap-snap pause before the next player has to name a movie on the slap-clap.

Obviously, longer names like *The Incredibly Strange Creatures Who Stopped Living and Became Mixed-up Zombies* are tricky to fit into two beats and you have to rattle through them really quickly. Hearing you deliver a tongue-twister can give the next player the giggles, causing him or her to mess up their answer. That player is then out of the game. A player is out if he or she loses the beat, gives a wrong answer, or gives an answer that has already been used—repeats are not allowed.

When a player is out, the next player begins again with a new topic—maybe sports cars, rock stars or wild animals. Once the players have each named two or three "in-sects," it becomes really difficult to think of another in time to deliver it without losing the beat.

PANTS ON FIRE

Ideally, you should have at least six players for this game, split into two or more teams of three.

What you will need:

• A dictionary • Pad of paper • A pen • A watch or clock

What you must do:

The first team has three minutes to look up an unusual word in the dictionary. They write the word down on a piece of paper. One player memorizes the true meaning of the word, and the other two have to make up silly definitions that are totally false.

The word is then revealed to the other team or teams, and each of the players in the first team presents their definition, giving a detailed explanation to persuade the opposition that they are telling the truth.

Once the others have made up their minds, they call on each of the first team to sum up their definition. As each states his or her answer, the opposition calls out "Liar, liar, pants on fire!" if they think the player is telling a big fat fib, or "True, true, it's you!"

The first team must then reveal who was telling the truth. The opposition gets a point if they guessed correctly but nothing if they got it wrong. The dictionary is then passed to the next team.

2+ PLAYERS

Pairs

For some card games, you need to learn complicated rules and know when it's time to make certain moves, but for this one, all you need is a good memory.

What you will need:

• A full deck of cards

What you must do:

Shuffle the cards thoroughly and then lay them out, face down, on a table in six neat rows with nine cards in each row—include the jokers. The game involves turning the cards over two at a time, so you need to leave a little bit of space between the cards when you lay them out.

The first player has to turn over two cards. If the cards are matching—two kings, two fives or two tens, for instance—the player keeps the two cards and takes another turn. If they do not match, the player turns the cards face down again, returning them to their original positions.

Everyone has to watch as the cards are turned over and try to remember where they are, so that when it comes to their turn, if the first card they turn over is a four, they will know where to find another four.

There won't be many pairs to begin with, but as the game progresses, there will be more and more. The winner is the player who has the most cards when all of the pairs have been picked up.

Shuffle the pack well before you start a new game.

Professor's tip:
Look for easy ways to help you remember where cards are. If a five is the fifth card in a row, or a three is in the third column, they are easier to remember.

BEETLE

You don't have to be a great artist for this game, and there's
no skill or strategy—it's all down to lucky numbers.

What you will need:

• A dice • Paper and a pencil for each player

What you must do:

The object of the game is to draw a beetle that has a specific number of body parts.
There is a body, six legs, a head, two feelers, and two eyes.

Players take turns rolling the dice. They must roll a 1 to get started. Rolling a 1 allows
them to draw the body. Without the body, they can't add any of the other parts.
It can take a few turns to roll a 1, but after that, they need the following:

A two for the head • A three for each of the two eyes • A four for each of the
two feelers • A five or a six for each of the six legs

The body must come first, but legs can be added to the body before the head.
Similarly, you have to have a head on your beetle before you can add eyes and feelers.

The first one to finish their beetle is the winner.

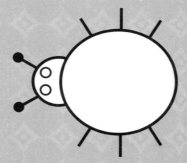

CUTTING THE LADY IN HALF

Cutting the lady in half is a stage magician's trick, but with a little preparation, you can do it in your own living room.

What you will need:

• A paper tube or envelope • A slip of paper
• A pencil • A pair of scissors

What you must do:

Draw your lady on the slip of paper. She will be your beautiful assistant and you should introduce her to the audience.

Now you need a paper tube big enough for your assistant to fit inside. You can make a tube by sealing an envelope and cutting off the ends. You need to do this in advance, so that you have your tube ready before you start doing the trick. This is because you need to make a couple of cuts in the tube. These need to be a little wider than your assistant because she needs to be able to fit through them.

Make the cuts across the back of your tube, so that they will always be facing away from the audience. You will give the trick away if anyone sees these sneaky slots.

The idea is that you will put your paper assistant into the tube and then cut the whole thing in half, yet your assistant will emerge completely unscathed. The trick is to slip your assistant into the tube with the front of the tube facing the audience. They will not see that you are actually slipping your assistant out through the first slot at the back, and then back in through the second slot.

As far as the audience is concerned, they will see your assistant's head sticking out of one end of the tube and her feet sticking out of the other. You then use the scissors to begin cutting the envelope, always making sure that your audience only sees the front of the tube. At the back of the tube, you have to slip the bottom blade of your scissors between the tube and your assistant, so that you are cutting through the tube but not the lovely lady.

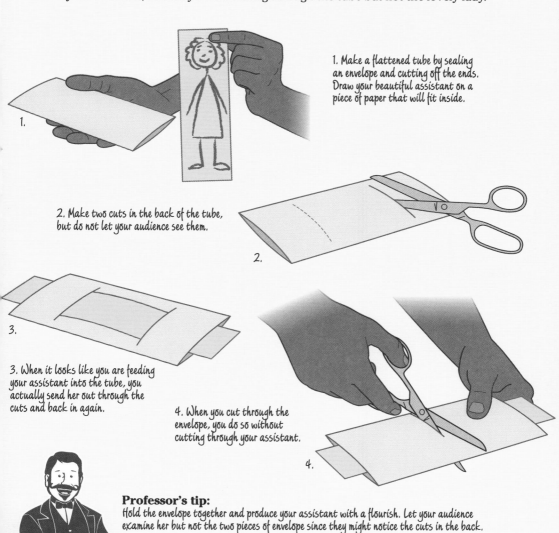

1. Make a flattened tube by sealing an envelope and cutting off the ends. Draw your beautiful assistant on a piece of paper that will fit inside.

2. Make two cuts in the back of the tube, but do not let your audience see them.

3. When it looks like you are feeding your assistant into the tube, you actually send her out through the cuts and back in again.

4. When you cut through the envelope, you do so without cutting through your assistant.

Professor's tip:
Hold the envelope together and produce your assistant with a flourish. Let your audience examine her but not the two pieces of envelope since they might notice the cuts in the back.

Stretch-A-Sketch

Even the world's greatest artists would struggle to create a decent sketch without being able to see what's farther up the page.

What you will need:

• A pencil • Paper

What you must do:

The players sit around a table, and the first player starts the sketch. You must all agree that you are drawing an animal, or an alien, or a soldier—something that starts off with a head, then has a body of some kind and ultimately legs and feet.

The first player starts with the head, and the last player knows that he or she will be finishing off with feet, or flippers, or whatever comes to mind. No one, however, is allowed to see what has gone before.

Being careful not to let anyone see what is being drawn, the first player sketches a head and then folds the paper back, so that the head is behind the blank paper with only a couple of little lines showing to let the next player know where to continue the sketch.

The second player folds the paper again, so that his or her contribution is also now behind the blank sheet and the next person continues the drawing from the ends of the lines left by the second player. So it continues until the last person completes the drawing and the previous stages are folded back to reveal the most bizarre sketch imaginable!

 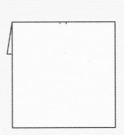 

HANGMAN

This is a battle of wits where you have to figure out the mystery word letter by letter, with every wrong guess taking you one step closer to losing.

What you will need:

• Paper • A pencil

What you must do:

The first player thinks of a word or phrase and marks it down on the paper as a series of dashes—one dash for each letter and a suitable space between words. The player gives one clue such as, "It's a country," or "It's a book title."

The others now take turns guessing letters that may be in the mystery word. A player is allowed to guess just one letter. If the letter is correct, the first player fills in the blanks where the letter appears. If it is not, the first player can start his scaffold, adding one line to the drawing every time there is a wrong guess—first the base, then the stand, the supports, and so on.

With the scaffold complete, the head, body, arms, legs, and feet of the man being hanged are added, one part for each wrong guess. The wrong letters are written down at the side, so that everyone knows what has already been guessed. If the feet are in place before the mystery word is guessed, the first player has won the game and can choose whether to have another turn or pass the paper to someone else.

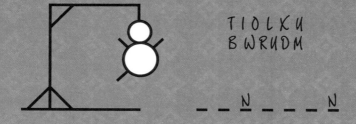

BLACKJACK

If you can count to 21, you have a good chance of
winning this game of luck and guesswork.

What you will need:

• A deck of cards • Something to bet with, such as tokens,
beads, or pieces of candy. You can even cut up small squares of paper
as tokens to make sure everyone has a dozen or so.

What you must do:

One person is nominated as the dealer. The dealer gives each player one
card, placed face down in front of them. The dealer gives himself or herself a card
last of all. Players look at their cards without letting anyone else see. The aim is
to collect cards that will add up to 21 or as close as you can get. Face cards
count as 10, and an ace can be either 1 or 11. Players then place bets on whether
they think they can get to 21. The minimum bet is one token, the maximum is
four, and all bets are placed in the middle of the table.

The dealer then gives everyone a second card, face down. Players study their
cards. A face card or a 10 and an ace would give 21—blackjack—and any player
who has a blackjack must say so. The dealer pays that player, and any other who
has a blackjack, twice what he or she bet, unless the dealer also has a blackjack,
in which case, the dealer wins and takes everything that has been bet.

If no one has a blackjack, the dealer asks each player one by one if they would
like another card and deals it face up. That card may take the player closer
to 21, and they can ask for another card if they wish. If they go over 21,
they are "bust" and out of the game.

A player close to 21 can choose to "stick"—take no more cards—and once
everyone has either stuck or bust, the dealer's cards are revealed. The dealer
then chooses to take more cards or to stick. If the dealer gets closest to 21,
the dealer wins. If the dealer goes bust, the player closest to 21 wins.

BUZZ

You have to keep your wits about you and know
your multiplication tables to keep up with this
fast-paced game.

What you must do:

The players sit in a circle or around a table. The first player
starts off saying "one," the next says "two," the next "three"
and so on around the table until you reach seven.
Instead of seven, you must say "buzz."

You must also say "buzz" on multiples of seven—14, 21, 28, 35 and
upward—as well as any number that has seven in it—17, 27, 37 and
upward. When you get to 77, you have to say "buzz-buzz."

If you say a number when you should say "buzz" or think about it
too long, you are out of the game. The last player left is the winner.

Professor's tip:
If it starts to get too easy only
using seven as buzz, then why
not also try buzzing on numbers
that are multiples of nine or
have nine in them?

Get Knotted!

Don't get yourself all tied up in knots when you try
this party trick—it's a lot easier than it seems.

What you will need:

• A standard square cloth table napkin

What you must do:

Tell your friends that you can pick a napkin up off the table, taking
an end in each hand, and tie a knot in the middle without letting go
of either end. They will not believe you, but here's how it's done.

Place the napkin on the table in front of you, neatly folded in a
triangle. Now stand in front of the napkin and fold your arms.
Without unfolding your arms, bend down to the left and grab the
left corner of the triangle in your right hand. Bend the other
way, and grab the right corner in your left hand.

Stand up straight and draw your arms apart, pulling your right
hand to the right and your left hand to the left, without letting
go of the napkin ends.

When your arms are completely unfolded, the napkin
will have a knot in the middle.

Professor's tip:
Trying to pick up the napkin feels really awkward at first, but once you
have done it a couple of times, it gets much easier.

TIC-TAC-TOE

If you play this game fast, you have to think fast, and
mistakes can be made that will cost you a win.

What you will need:

• Two pencils

What you must do:

Draw two horizontal and two vertical lines that intersect to form a grid of nine squares.

Decide who will go first, who will be X, and who will be O. If you are X,
your aim is to get three Xs in a row horizontally, vertically, or diagonally.
If you are O, you want three Os.

If X goes first, the player puts an X in one of the boxes. Some like to
start by taking the center box, but that does not guarantee you victory.
O then marks a box. X must now mark a second box, and O needs to
make sure that the next O blocks X from making a line of three.

So it continues, until someone gets three in a row or all the squares are full.
Take turns going first, and play fast to make it more likely that your
opponent will make a mistake and let you in for three in a row.

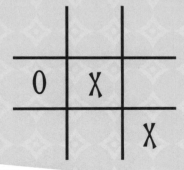

32

BATTLESHIPS

2+
PLAYERS

Destroy your enemy's fleet without leaving
the comfort of your own living room.

What you will need:

• Pencil and paper for each player

What you must do:

Each player marks out two 10 x 10 grids. Down the left, the rows are
numbered 1 to 10. Across the top, the columns are lettered A to J.
One grid is labeled "Home Fleet," the other "Enemy Fleet."

On the "Home Fleet" grid, you must now deploy your ships without
letting your enemy see. Each player has one battleship that covers
four squares, two cruisers (three squares each), three destroyers
(two squares each), and four submarines (one square each).
Your ships must be marked horizontally or vertically,
not diagonally, and must not be touching.

Decide who goes first, and then take turns firing at your enemy's
ships by calling out a square using a grid reference. F6, for example,
is column F, row 6. If part of an enemy ship occupies that square,
the other player must call out "Hit!" If it is an empty square, the call is
"Miss!" If you score a hit, your opponent must tell you what you have hit,
and you get to have another turn. If it's a miss, it's his turn to fire at you.

You need four hits to sink a battleship, three to sink a cruiser,
two for a destroyer, and one for a sub. The first one to sink all
their enemy's ships is the winner.

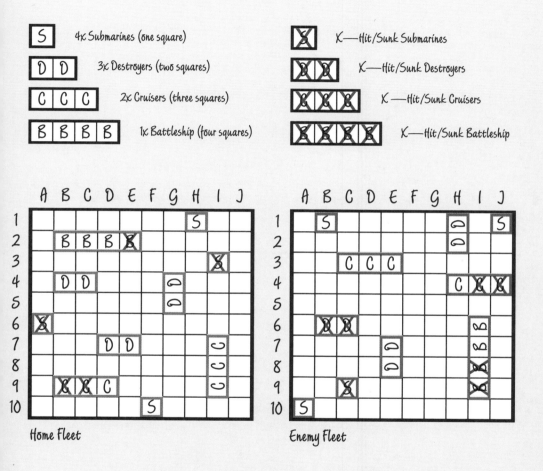

	4x Submarines (one square)
	3x Destroyers (two squares)
	2x Cruisers (three squares)
	1x Battleship (four squares)

X—Hit/Sunk Submarines
X—Hit/Sunk Destroyers
X—Hit/Sunk Cruisers
X—Hit/Sunk Battleship

Home Fleet

Enemy Fleet

Professor's tip:
If you score a "miss," remember to mark it on your Enemy Fleet grid. Shade the square or write "M" for miss, so that you know there is no ship in that square and you won't fire at it again.

Picture This

There is no quiet way to play this game, so be prepared for a lively, noisy time and lots of laughs!

What you will need:

• Pencil and paper • A clock or watch

What you must do:

This game is like Charades (see p10). The player trying to convey the title of a book, play, movie, song, or TV show can't make a sound and is not allowed to make any gestures or do any acting. Instead, they have to draw clues on a piece of paper.

Players are divided into two teams, and one team must write down a title. This is then given to one of the players from the other team, who must not show the title to the rest of his or her team.

Using a different sheet of paper, the player has to draw a book, a stage with curtains, a movie camera, a singing face, or a TV to give the team its first clue.

The player then marks a series of dashes on the paper, one for each letter of the title, with a / to show a break between words.

The player points to a word, or even a letter, and draws something to represent that word. If the title was *Charlie and the Chocolate Factory*, the player could show that it was a book, a movie, and a play, point to the last word, and try to draw a factory.

Players have to be quick on the draw, because they have just five minutes to get their team to come up with the answer. After that, the other team gets a turn. The team with the most correct answers at the end of the evening is the winner.

STRING RELAY

In most races, you need strong legs and stamina to come first, but this race relies more on nimble fingers.

What you will need:

• Two pieces of string
(the more players you have, the longer the strings need to be)

What you must do:

Nominate a Starter who will say "Go!" to start the relay race. The players are divided into two relay teams and must sit on the floor or at a table in a line.

The first player in each team holds their piece of string, and when the starter calls "Go!" player 1 ties a knot in the string and passes it to player 2, who does the same.

The last player ties a knot, and the string is passed all the way back to the first player, who unties one knot. One by one, each player unties a knot, and the last player passes the untied string back to player 1.

The first team to have a knot-free piece of string back in the hands of their first player is the winner.

Professor's tip:
Don't get overexcited and tie your knots too tight, or it will take forever to untie them again.

VANISHING COTTON SWAB

Make an ordinary cotton swab disappear from your
hand right in front of your audience!

What you will need:

• A cotton swab • Scissors
• A small piece of double-sided tape

What you must do:

This magic trick can be performed with your audience quite close, but you
must keep your hands moving and keep talking to distract their attention.

The one piece of preparation that you have to do is to attach the
double-sided tape to the thumbnail on your right hand.
Trim the tape so that it neatly covers your thumbnail.

Show the cotton swab to your audience, holding it in your left hand and
keeping your hands on the move. You don't want anyone to see that tape.
You can even give the cotton swab to someone in the audience to inspect,
so that they know it is a real cotton swab.

Then, holding the cotton swab in your left hand, place it in your right hand
as though you are gripping it in your fist. The audience will still see the
top of the cotton swab sticking up, but they will not see your right thumb
folded down behind your fingers, with your fingers pressing the swab
against the tape.

Don't hold the swab like that for more than a moment or two; otherwise,
someone may notice that your thumb is in a strange place. Distract the
audience by talking and waving your left hand aound, then slap your left

hand into your right fist and quickly open both hands, showing the palms outward to your audience. The cotton swab will appear to have gone, but it is actually hidden behind your right thumb.

Wave your hands around, keeping your palms toward the audience, and snatch your right hand down in front of you, forming a fist as before to make it look like you have just plucked the swab out of the air.

You can use your left hand quickly to pull the swab off the tape, then hand it back to one of your amazed audience.

1.

1. Put double-sided tape on your thumbnail. The neater you make it, the less obvious it will be.

2.

2. When you have put the cotton swab in your right hand, keep your left hand moving to distract the audience.

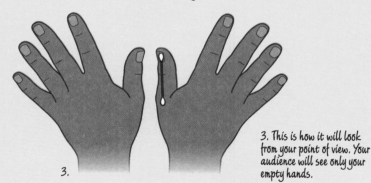

3.

3. This is how it will look from your point of view. Your audience will see only your empty hands.

Professor's tip:
Keep your hands on the move to distract your audience's attention, but be careful not to let them see behind your thumb where the cotton swab is hiding.

WORD RACE

You have to be able to spell simple words to take part in this game, and be able to spot places to create them.

What you will need:

• Paper and pencils for each player • A dictionary (optional)

What you must do:

Each player writes down all of the letters of the alphabet on his or her sheet of paper. A ten-square by ten-square grid is then drawn on a separate sheet.

The first player then writes a word horizontally as close to the middle of the grid as possible. You can only use letters from your alphabet (so no double letters), and you check off the letters as you use them so you can't use them again.

The next player then writes a word vertically that intersects with the first word. Words must always intersect, and players continue to take turns. If you can't think of a word to use, you miss a turn.

Play continues until someone wins by using up all of his or her letters, but it is more likely that you will reach the stage where no one can think of a word using the letters they have left. Once you agree to call a halt, the player with the fewest letters left wins.

ABCDEFG
HIJKLMNO
PQRSTUV
WXYZ

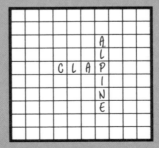

ABCDEFG
HIJKLMNO
PQRSTUV
WXYZ

2+ PLAYERS

CAR CODES

When you get stuck in traffic on a long and tedious car trip, this game is silly enough to raise a few smiles.

What you will need:

• A traffic jam • A clock or watch

What you must do:

One person in the car is nominated as the Chief Codebreaker and the Chief Codebreaker points out the license plates of nearby cars to each player, or Spy.

The Spy must study the letters of the license plate (ignore the numbers) and figure out a coded message they might represent—the sillier the better.

For example, a license plate that has letters in the order PFD could be "Partly Full Donuts" or "Pants Falling Down."

If a Spy fails to come up with a coded message within 20 seconds, as timed by the Chief Codebreaker, he or she is out, and the winner is the last Spy left. The last Spy then becomes the new Chief Codebreaker, and you start all over again.

LORD OF THE RING

2+ PLAYERS

If you have good aim and a steady hand, you can become the Lord (or Lady!) of the Ring in this classic marbles game.

What you will need:

- Marbles—three for each player
- A piece of thread or a sheet of newspaper

What you must do:

Each player is given three marbles. If they are all the same color or pattern, that is good but not vital.

A circle needs to be marked on the ground. If you are outside, scratch a rough circle with a stick in the dirt to make a target ring. If you are playing inside, you can arrange the piece of thread on the floor to make a target ring. If you don't have any thread, lay down a sheet of newspaper to make your target area.

Each player then puts one marble inside the ring, positioning it wherever they like. The players then take turns "shooting" one of their remaining marbles at the marbles in the ring. You can shoot by flicking the marble out of your hand with your thumb or by rolling it along the ground. You must all shoot from the same point an agreed distance from the ring.

The object is to knock one of more of the marbles out of the ring. Players keep any marbles that they knock out of the ring. If you shoot and miss, you can collect your shooting marble from wherever it lands, unless it stops inside the ring, in which case you must leave it there. When you next shoot, you will then have to use one of your other marbles until you are down to your last one. Lose that, and you are out of the game.

The winner is the player who ends up with the most marbles when there are none left in the ring.

TWENTY QUESTIONS

Telling the truth but still keeping your secret is a real challenge when you are faced with questioners determined to find out what you are thinking.

What you must do:

The aim of the game is to find out a secret word that one of the players is thinking. The other players are allowed to ask questions, to figure out the secret word, but if they can't guess it after 20 questions have been asked, the player with the secret wins the game.

One player has to be selected to start and must think of a word. It can be something in the room, something from the outside world, an animal, a car, a movie star—anything at all.

The others then take turns asking questions. At first, the questions need to be very general in order to get them thinking along the right lines: "Is it a living thing?" for example, or "Is it a machine?"

The player with the secret is only allowed to answer yes or no. No other clues can be given. If the answer to "Is it a living thing?" was yes, then the next question might be "Is it an animal?" followed by "Does it live on a farm?"

When one of the players thinks he or she knows what the secret word is, that player's next question should be a guess, such as, "Is it a donkey?" If the guess is wrong, that player is out of the game for the remainder of the round. If the guess is right, that player is the winner and is the next one to think of a secret word.

DISSOLVING COIN

Can a coin magically dissolve beneath an empty wine glass?
If you can perfect this trick, then of course it can!

What you will need:

• A wine glass • A coin • Three identical sheets of colored paper
• A pencil • Scissors • Double-sided tape • A cloth

What you must do:

This trick requires careful secret preparation and a little practice if you are to make it work flawlessly. The first thing that you have to do is to prepare your wine glass. Place the glass upside down on one of your identical sheets of colored paper, and draw around it very carefully with a sharp pencil.

You will be left with a circle on the paper. Cut out this circle, making sure that you follow the line precisely. Now cut four thin pieces of double-sided tape. You should aim to make them no wider than the thickness of the rim of the wine glass.

Stick the tape to the rim of the glass. If there is any excess, either trim it off or make sure that it folds up inside the glass. It shouldn't show if there is only a tiny amount. You should position the tape at four points around the rim—where 12, 3, 6, and 9 would be on a clock face.

Now press the rim down onto the disk of colored paper that you cut out. The rim should fit exactly over the disk. When you stand the wine glass on its base, it should look like illustration 2.

You are now ready to set up your trick. Your audience must not see that the mouth of the wine glass is covered with colored paper, so you have to set up the trick in advance, perhaps on a tray that you can carry into the room.

You should have two sheets of colored paper lying side by side. The wine glass stands upside down on one sheet, and on the other sheet, you place an ordinary coin.

Cover the wine glass with a cloth and say your favorite magic words before you pick it up—still covered with the cloth, so that the audience can't see the colored paper stuck to it—and place it on the other sheet of paper.

With a few more magic words and hand waving, you can remove the cloth and the wine glass will be standing in place, but the coin will appear to have vanished, although actually it is just hidden beneath the paper that you stuck to the wine glass.

2. Cut out the disk of colored paper, so that it can be stuck neatly over the top of the glass.

1. Carefully draw around the upturned glass as accurately as you can.

3. When the upturned glass sits on a fresh sheet of colored paper, the disk will not be noticed.

4. Cover the glass with a napkin before you move it, and when you remove the napkin, the disk will be hiding the coin as though it has vanished.

Professor's tip:
The essential thing is to cut and attach the disk neatly. Any rough edges will be noticed when the glass is standing on one of the other sheets of colored paper.

BLINDMAN'S BLUFF

A little clear floor space is required for this game to make sure that your "blindman" (or woman) doesn't go crashing into the furniture.

What you will need:

• A blindfold

What you must do:

One player is chosen to be the first to wear the blindfold. Once blindfolded, the player is spun around three times, and everyone else scatters out of reach.

The blindfolded player now staggers around the room trying to catch hold of any of the other players. The other players move around, make as much noise as they like, give the blindfolded player false directions, and can even dart in to tickle or gently tug a sleeve if they are brave enough to risk being caught.

When the blindfolded player catches someone, the captured player must not speak, since the one wearing the blindfold has to identify his prisoner by touch alone.

If the blindfolded player guesses correctly, the captured player takes the blindfold and the game starts again. If he or she guesses wrongly, the prisoner is released and the "blindman" has to catch someone else.

2+ PLAYERS

CENTURY

Keeping track of your score requires a little arithmetic, and that helps to sharpen your wits!

What you will need:

• Two dice • Pencil and paper

What you must do:

Players take turns throwing the dice and adding up their score each time they throw. They throw both dice at once and have only one throw per turn.

If they score a double, that score counts as double, so two fives will count as 20, not 10.

Each player keeps his or her own score on a piece of paper, and the first one to reach 100 is the winner.

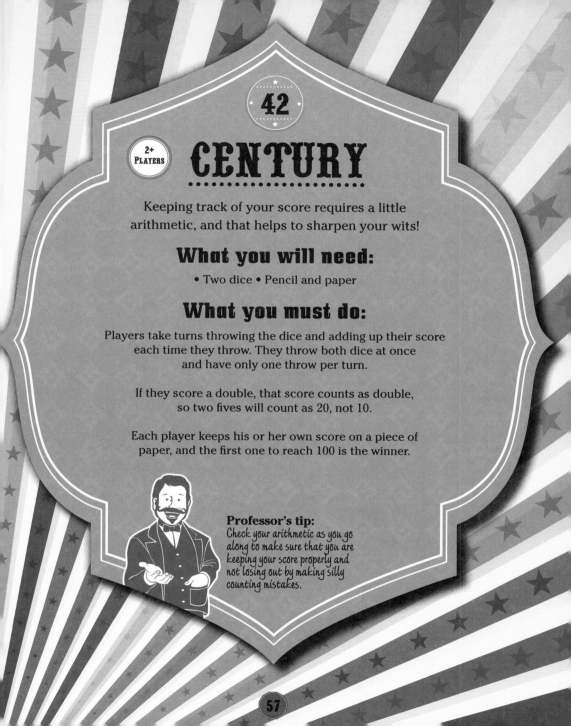

Professor's tip:
Check your arithmetic as you go along to make sure that you are keeping your score properly and not losing out by making silly counting mistakes.

Millennium

Like the Century game on the previous page, Millennium involves keeping count of the score, but this time the numbers are bigger.

What you will need:

• Six dice • Pencil and paper

What you must do:

Players take turns throwing the dice. A player throws all six dice at once and scores only if the dice show a sequence or multiple numbers. Players earn points for rolling sequences or multiples as follows:

Sequence of three (1, 2, 3 or 2, 3, 4 or 3, 4, 5 or 4, 5, 6)	250 points
Sequence of four (1, 2, 3, 4 or 2, 3, 4, 5 or 3, 4, 5, 6)	500 points
Sequence of five (1, 2, 3, 4, 5 or 2, 3, 4, 5, 6)	750 points
Sequence of six	1,000 points
Three of a kind	250 points
Four of a kind	500 points
Five of a kind	750 points
Six of a kind	1,000 points

It is possible on one roll to be able to count more than one score—a sequence of three and three of a kind, for instance. If this happens, you count both scores. A sequence of three and three of a kind would score 500 points. A sequence of four and three of a kind would score 750.

First player to reach 1,000 points or more is the winner.

Professor's tip:
Keep up with the scoring to make sure that everyone is writing down their score correctly. It's easy to make mistakes with big numbers when things are moving quickly.

WHO'S AT THE PARTY?

It's a strange kind of party where everyone knows everyone else, but none of the guests know who they are!

What you will need:

• Pencil • Sticky notes (or paper and tape)

What you must do:

Each player must write the name of a famous person—or a character from a book, play, song, movie, or TV show—on a sticky note without anyone seeing what they have written. They each then stick the name to the forehead of the player next to them, without letting that player see what the name is.

When everyone has a name on their forehead, everyone can see everyone else's name, but not their own. Players must take turns asking a question about "themselves," such as "Am I a man?" or "Am I on TV?" or "Do I have red hair?" The other players shout out yes or no. If the answer is yes, the player immediately gets to ask another question, if not, it is the next player's turn to ask about himself or herself.

When a player has asked enough questions to know that she is a female singer who has also appeared in movies and is still in the news, the player might want to use their next question to guess "Am I Madonna?" If that's the name on the sticky note then that player has won, but the game goes on until everyone has guessed who they are.

Catch the Queen

You can fool a friend with this simple party trick once, but the queen probably won't escape a second time.

2+ Players

What you will need:

- Four ordinary playing cards, including one queen
- A paper clip • Some glue or tape (optional)

What you must do:

Arrange the cards as shown in the first illustration, with the queen in the middle. To make it easier for you when you are showing people this trick, you might want to put a few blobs of glue on the cards or use some tape to hold them together in this formation. This isn't part of the trick, and you can show everyone that the cards are stuck together—or even tell everyone that sticking the cards together means that there's no way you can secretly switch them around.

Show your audience the cards face out, so that they can see that the queen is in the middle, then turn the cards around; so that they can see only the backs.

Now ask for a volunteer, hand your volunteer the paper clip and ask him or her to "catch the queen" by putting a paper clip over the queen. Most people will, at first, choose the middle card, as seen from the back, and place the clip as shown in the second illustration.

When you turn the cards around to face your audience again, the paper clip will be over the end card, as in the final illustration, not the middle card, and it will look like your volunteer missed the queen by miles!

1. Show the cards with the queen clearly visible in the middle.

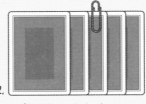

2. When shown the backs, most people will clip the middle card.

3. Turn the cards back to show they've totally missed the queen.

THREE-IN-A-ROW

There's an element of skill involved in this game, but your skill develops quickly after just a few sessions.

What you will need:

• Paper and pencil • Six counters—two different-colored sets of three

What you must do:

Draw your Three-in-a-Row board on a piece of paper by copying the diagram shown here.

When you have decided who will go first, that player places a counter at a point on the board where lines intersect. The other player then places a counter at a different intersection. The aim is to get three counters in a row and to stop your opponent from getting three in a row. In that respect, this is a little like tic-tac-toe.

If no one has won once both players have placed all three of their counters, they then take turns moving one counter along a line to the next intersection, in any direction, provided that the intersection is not already occupied. They still need three in a row to win. If you reach the stage where no one can make a move, the game is a tie.

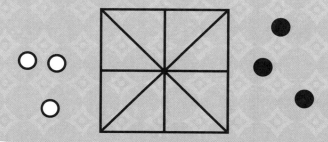

WORD LADDERS

This is a traditional game that requires a little thought and is very rewarding when you make it work.

What you will need:

• Paper and pencil for each player • A watch or clock

What you must do:

This is a race with each player competing to be first to finish the word ladder, not in the least time but in the least number of steps. If the challenge is, for example, to change COW to PIG, one letter at a time, creating a new word at each stage, one solution is COW–COG–DOG–DIG–PIG.

The words must all have the same number of letters, and the minimum number of steps on your word ladder is the same as the number of letters in the word. You may often, however, need to take much more than the minimum number of steps.

It is more fun to choose first and last words that have some type of link, like SEED and TREE (SEED–SLED–FLED–FLEE–FREE–TREE) or BOY to MAN (BOY–BAY–MAY–MAN).

Although the first person to find a solution may not have found the most direct route—BOY to MAN could be BOY–TOY–TON–TAN–MAN, one step more than above—you can't wait around forever trying to figure out the shortest route, so it's best to set a time limit of five minutes.

If no one can find a solution after five minutes, set another word ladder challenge.

| COW |
| COG |
| DOG |
| DIG |
| PIG |

| SEED |
| SLED |
| FLED |
| FLEE |
| FREE |
| TREE |

THE MAGIC STRAW

Make a straw spin on a bottle cap without touching it.

What you will need:

• A plastic drinking straw • A plastic bottle with
the cap in place • Wool sweater or fleece

What you must do:

Rub the drinking straw on your sweater, swiping
it several times. Only touch the straw with one
hand, and hold it at one end.

Now balance the straw on top of the bottle, and
immediately move your hand away.

Move a finger close to the straw, and it will start
to move toward your finger. Move your finger
around the bottle, and the straw will spin on top.
Be gentle, or the straw may fall off the bottle, but
do not let the straw touch your finger.

Rubbing the straw creates static electricity
and gives the straw a negative electrical
charge. When you hold your finger
close to the end of the straw, the
straw is attracted to the positive
charge on your skin in the same
way that opposite ends of a
magnet are attracted.

Clip the Clips

Use this easy trick to join two paper clips together without touching either one.

What you will need:

• A banknote or a piece of paper in the shape of a banknote • Two paperclips

What you must do:

The first thing to do is to show your audience the banknote, so that they can see it is perfectly ordinary. If you can borrow the note from someone in the audience, that's even better.

Now fold the note in a loose zigzag so that you have three edges along the top as in diagram 1. Your paper clips now have to be slipped onto the banknote so that one is clipping the front of the note to the middle and the other is clipping the back of the note to the middle.

You can now announce that you will join the two clips together without touching either one. Grip each end of the banknote as shown in diagram 2.

Finally, you pull the note sharply open, so that it is entirely flat and unfolded. The paper clips will spring off the top of the note, and as if by magic, they will be neatly linked together.

1. Place the clips to hold the note in a zigzag shape.

2. With the clips in place, grip the ends of the note firmly.

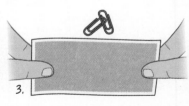

3. Pull sharply open, and the clips will ping off, locked together.

ALPHABET MARKET

You will have some strange items on
your shopping list by the end of this game!

What you will need:

• A good memory

What you must do:

Gather everyone around in a circle on the floor or seated
around a table, and decide who's going to start. If you play
a few different rounds, you can take turns starting.

The first player begins by saying, "I went to the market and bought a …" and
must list something beginning with the letter A. The next player must list
something beginning with B, but also has to say what the item beginning
with A was, and so on, working your way through the alphabet.

Player 1: I went to the market and bought an … apricot.
Player 2: I went to the market and bought an apricot and a bag.
Player 3: I went to the market and bought an apricot, a bag, and a chicken.
Player 4: I went to the market and bought an apricot, a bag, a chicken, and a donkey.

Remembering everything that has gone before becomes harder as the game
goes on. If you can't remember, or recite the list wrongly, you're out of that
round. The last person left in the game is the winner.

Professor's tip:
If you try to picture each item in your head when it is mentioned,
you can use that mental image to help you remember it.

JUMPING RUBBER BAND

Make a rubber band jump across your hand.

2+ PLAYERS

What you will need:

• A rubber band

What you must do:

This party trick looks really slick, but it is actually very easy to master. Hold up one hand to your audience, turning it to show them the palm and the back of your hand so that they can see you are not hiding any kind of device or any other rubber bands.

With the back of your hand facing the audience, place a rubber band over your pinkie and ring finger. Keep the back of your hand to the audience and pull the band tight with your free hand, telling the audience that the band is tight, it's not broken, and it can't slip off.

What you are actually doing is dragging the rubber band open into the palm of your hand. You then quickly curl your fingers into a clenched fist, so that all of your fingertips are inside the band, then release the band as you unclench your fingers.

The rubber band will have jumped from your pinkie and ring finger to your middle and forefinger.

With a little practice, you can make the "jump" happen very quickly and very smoothly, so that even if your audience is very close, from their perspective looking at the back of your hand, they won't be able to tell how you did it.

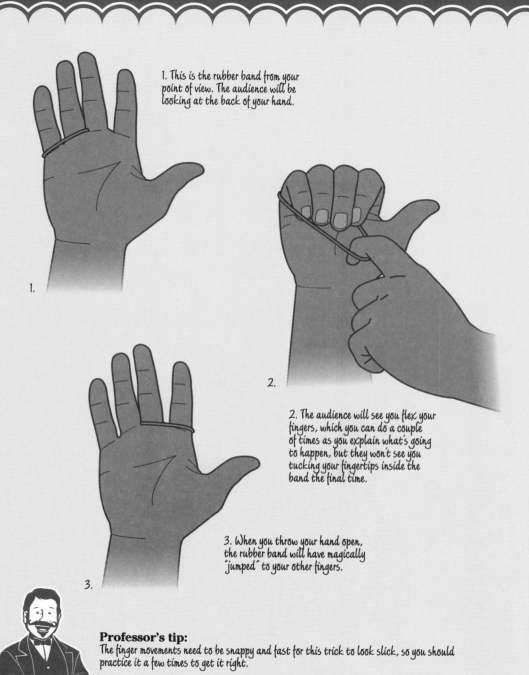

1. This is the rubber band from your point of view. The audience will be looking at the back of your hand.

1.

2.

2. The audience will see you flex your fingers, which you can do a couple of times as you explain what's going to happen, but they won't see you tucking your fingertips inside the band the final time.

3. When you throw your hand open, the rubber band will have magically "jumped" to your other fingers.

3.

Professor's tip:
The finger movements need to be snappy and fast for this trick to look slick, so you should practice it a few times to get it right.

BOXES

In this game, the winner comes last.

What you will need:

• As many toothpicks as you can find

What you must do:

Create a grid of toothpick boxes, laying the toothpicks out horizontally and vertically to make as big a grid as you can. You should aim to have a grid at least five boxes wide and five boxes high—for that, you will need 60 toothpicks.

Each player then takes a turn picking up toothpicks from the grid. You can pick up one toothpick, or you can pick up two if they are touching.

The last player to pick up a toothpick is the winner.

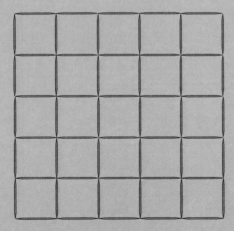

53 LEG LISTS

2+ PLAYERS

How many things can you think of that have legs?

What you will need:

• A sheet of paper • A pencil • Scissors

What you must do:

Write down the letters of the alphabet from A to Z and then cut them out, so that you have 26 scraps of paper, each with a letter on it.

Turn the letters face down in the middle of a table, and mix them all up.

The first player picks a letter from the pile and must name something beginning with that letter that has legs. If the first player picks the letter "P," then he or she might say "Panda." The next player must also name something beginning with P that has legs—piano, pig, parrot, policeman or pterodactyl are a few examples. The round continues with each person naming something beginning with P that has legs.

If a player can't come up with an answer or gives an answer that has already been given, that player is out of the round. The winner of the round is the last player left, and that player keeps the letter. He or she then chooses the next letter, and the game begins again.

The player with the most letters at the end of the game is the winner.

THE FLOATING CARD

Make a playing card hover in midair above your hand!

What you will need:

• Two playing cards • A craft knife • Some glue

What you must do:

Like so many magic tricks, to perform this one successfully, you have to do your best to distract your audience. By talking to them constantly and keeping your hands on the move, you will give them no chance of seeing how you are making the card float above the palm of your hand.

You must also prepare very carefully for this trick to create your special floating card. You need to use a craft knife to cut a flap in the middle of a playing card. The card will stand on this flap when you are making it look like it is floating, so the flap needs to be long enough to hold the card clear of your hand, but not so long that it will be noticed when you have it in the "closed" position.

Once you have cut the flap and bent it up, spread some glue over the face of the card. Be careful not to get any glue close to the flap area. Then, with the flap in the "open" position, stick your card to the back of another identical card. It doesn't have to be the same suit or number, but it should have the same decoration on the back and be exactly the same size—in other words, another card from the same deck.

Leave the flap open and allow the glue to dry completely. When the glue is dry, you can close the flap and practice showing the card to your audience. You can show them the card front and back, so that they can see it is an ordinary playing card. Hold a finger or thumb over the flap to keep it closed. The pattern on the back of most playing cards will help to disguise the cut lines.

Having shown the card to the audience, perhaps even having made it look as though you took it from a normal deck of cards, you then take the card and move it around over the palm of your hand as though you are tempting it to hover. What you are actually doing is manipulating the flap into the open position and gripping the very end of it between the fingers of your open palm.

You will have to practice how you show the card "hovering." It needs to be low down so that the audience can't see the flap. Keep your free hand on the move, swirling it around the card to distract the audience.

Finish the trick by snapping up the card with your free hand and secretly closing the flap before you give your audience another brief view of the card, front and back. Then put it away with the rest of the deck of cards before anyone can find out what makes your floating card so special.

1. Use a craft knife to cut the flap, and cut it at an angle so that the card will "hover" at an angle over your hand.

2. Stick the card to the back of another playing card that has an identical pattern on the back.

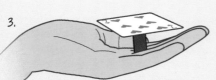

3. When you place the card in your flat palm, secretly open the flap and trap it between your fingers.

4. Hold the card at an angle to your audience so that they can see it is "floating" above your palm but can't see the flap underneath.

Professor's tip:
When preparing this trick, make sure that there is no glue under the flap and that you keep the flap open until the glue is completely dry.

Impossible Paper

Turn a sheet of paper into a shape that can't possibly exist!

2+ PLAYERS

What you will need:

• One sheet of paper • A pair of scissors

What you must do:

Take a look at the piece of paper in the first diagram. There is a single flap sticking up in the middle and a slot on either side, but the flap can't possibly have come from either of the slots. It's not an optical illusion or a trick drawing. You can actually make this seemingly impossible piece of paper—but if you challenge anyone else to do it, they won't know where to start.

To begin with, you need to fold your paper to mark eight equal segments. Fold it in half lengthwise, then open it out. Fold it in half the other way, then in half again, and open it out, so that you now have eight segments marked on your sheet.

On one side, make two cuts from the edge into the middle, separating the end segments from the middle two. On the other side, make one cut from the edge to the middle, cutting this side of the paper exactly in half.

You now have two cuts on one side of the paper and one cut on the other. You must now flip one half of the sheet as shown in illustration 3, then lay the sheet flat on the table in front of you.

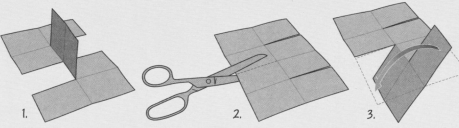

1. This paper shape looks like it is impossible to create from one sheet.

2. Cut accurately along the fold lines only as far as the middle.

3. Flip one side to create the shape that looks like it's impossible.

HOT AND COLD

Younger children love this game because
it gets very noisy!

What you will need:

• A small object to hide—pieces of candy are good
because you can eat them when you find them.

What you must do:

One player is sent out of the room, and the others choose a hiding
place for the object. When they have hidden it, they all call out
"Come and find it!" and the player comes back into the room.

The player then makes his way around the room, looking for the
hidden object. The others help by calling out "Cold!" if the seeker
is far away from the object, "Colder!" if the seeker moves farther
away, or "Freezing!" if the player is still going wrong.

On the other hand, if the player is getting close, the others
call out "Warm," "Warmer," "Hot," or "Scorching!"

When the object is found, another player is chosen
to step outside, and the game begins again.

Professor's tip:
Have fun when calling out directions by using as many different
"hot" and "cold" words as you can, such as "roasting" amd
"sunburned" or "arctic" and "snowman."

INDESTRUCTIBLE STRING

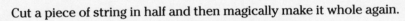

Cut a piece of string in half and then magically make it whole again.

What you will need:

- A drinking straw • A piece of string
- A pair of scissors • A craft knife

What you must do:

To perform this magic trick, you have to show your audience an ordinary drinking straw that has a piece of string or thread running through it. You should thread the string through the straw when you prepare this trick in advance because that can turn out to be the trickiest part of the trick.

Feeding the string through the straw can take time, but it is not the first stage of your preparations. Your first task is to cut a slit in the straw about 1 inch long very carefully. When you show the straw to your audience, you must keep this slit at the back, so that they can't see it.

With the slit cut and the string in place, you can show everyone that it is an ordinary straw and even let them tug on the string, so that they can see it is intact and runs all the way through.

Then, holding the straw in one hand, bend the top over, so that you are folding the straw in half. You will need to keep the bottom edges of the slit concealed behind a finger as you hold the straw. Grip both edges of the string in your free hand, and give them a little tug. Explain to your audience that you are just showing them that the string is still in there and still intact.

What you are actually doing is tugging the string out through the slot, so that the part of the straw where it is folded in half now has no string inside it.

You can now pick up your scissors and cut the straw in half at the fold, without cutting the string.

Everyone will be able to see that the straw has been cut in half, but now you must straighten it out again, hold it in the middle where you have just cut it in half, and with a flourish, pull the string out.

You can let your audience examine the string to show them that it is all in one piece, but crumple up the two pieces of straw and slip them into your pocket or a trash can, so that no one can find the slit.

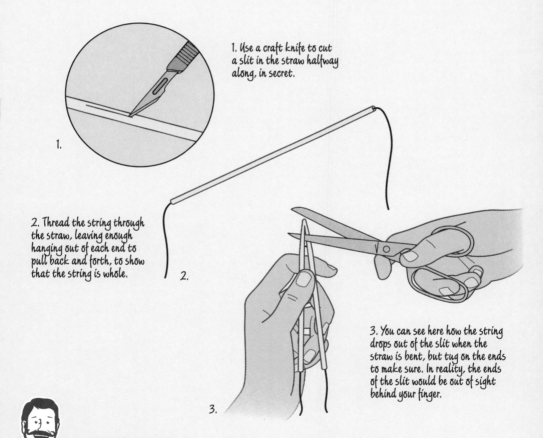

1. Use a craft knife to cut a slit in the straw halfway along, in secret.

1.

2. Thread the string through the straw, leaving enough hanging out of each end to pull back and forth, to show that the string is whole.

2.

3. You can see here how the string drops out of the slit when the straw is bent, but tug on the ends to make sure. In reality, the ends of the slit would be out of sight behind your finger.

3.

Professor's tip:
Let the audience touch the string inside the straw, even tug on the ends, but you must keep hold of the straw and keep the slit out of sight.

MURDER IN THE DARK

Can the detective uncover the evil villain
before another murder is committed?

What you will need:

• A deck of cards

What you must do:

Count out one card for each player, including the ace of diamonds
and the ace of spades. Give one card to each player.

The player who gets the ace of diamonds is the detective and the
only one who can reveal his card. The player who gets the ace of
spades is the murderer and must keep it a secret. The detective then
leaves the room and the lights are switched off, so that people are
moving around in complete darkness.

The murderer taps a victim three times on the shoulder. The victim
screams and falls to the floor. Everyone freezes except the murderer,
who can move away. The detective waits ten seconds, then enters
and switches on the light. He then questions witnesses, asking them
if they felt anyone moving around, or who they think the murderer is.
He can ask six questions.

Everyone must tell the truth, except the murderer. The detective
can ask anyone "Are you the murderer?" but can only ask this once.
If the person is not the murderer, the detective has lost.
The cards are then dealt again to start a new game.

CRAZY EIGHTS

In this game you win by losing all your cards.

What you will need:

• A deck of cards • Pencil and paper

What you must do:

The dealer deals five cards to each player. The rest are placed in a stack, face down, and the top card is turned over to start a "matching card" pile. If this card is an 8, it must be put back in the middle of the deck and the top card turned over again.

The aim is to discard all of your cards, one at a time, onto the matching cards pile. The player to the dealer's left begins. You have to be able to match the number or the suit of the card on top of the matching cards pile. If you don't have a matching card to discard, you have to take a card off the top of the deck.

If you have an 8, you can play it at any time and ask for the suit to be changed to whatever you want. For instance, if you have a lot of spades in your hand, you should choose spades.

The winner is the first person to discard all of their cards.

Self-slicing Banana

Peel a banana to reveal that it is already sliced inside.

2+ PLAYERS

What you will need:

• A fresh banana • A long pin

What you must do:

Amaze your friends with this party trick, having first done just a little preparation. Offer to share a banana with someone, telling them, "Don't worry, this banana comes pre-sliced." When you peel it—or you let your friend peel it—the banana will indeed be cut into slices inside its skin.

For the trick to work, the banana obviously has to look like no one has tampered with it. There should be no trace of any cut marks on the skin and the banana won't have been peeled already.

To achieve the magically sliced banana effect, you need to use a long pin—an ordinary pin of the type that you might find in a sewing kit. There are ridges on the skin of a banana, and as the banana ripens, these can take on a darker, brown color.

Push the pin into the banana through one of the ridges, preferably at a dark spot. Move the pin from side to side as you push it in, so that the pin under the skin gradually cuts through the banana.

Feel for when the pin inside the banana touches the inside of the banana skin to the left or right or at the other side of the banana, as you do not want to risk puncturing the skin.

1. Prepare beforehand by using a long pin to slice your banana. 2. Push the pin in through the ridges on the banana to ensure the holes aren't noticed. 3. Repeat the process several times, so that you can peel a presliced banana.

WORD LINKS

2+ PLAYERS

Quick thinking is required to build a
long chain of linked words.

What you must do:

One player starts by saying a word. The next player has to
call out a word that is linked to that word or associated with
it in some way. A typical linked chain might go as follows:

Player 1: Ball

Player 2: Foot

Player 3: Sock

Player 4: Smelly

Player 5: Uncle

At this point, one of the other players might call "Challenge"
because they see no obvious link between "Smelly" and
"Uncle." Player 5 can say that he has an uncle who works in
a cheese store and it's really smelly.

Everyone else must decide whether that is an acceptable link.
If it's not, then Player 5 drops out of the game. If it is,
then whoever called "Challenge" is out of the game.

The last player left is the winner.

Professor's tip:
Think fast but try not to suggest links that only you
can really understand because others might not be
ready to accept them.

MONEY MATTERS

This trick uses two banknotes, and what matters
is which one comes out on top.

What you will need:

• Two banknotes or two pieces of paper roughly the same size as banknotes

What you must do:

Make sure that the banknotes are different or that the pieces of paper
are different colors. If your two notes look identical, it will be difficult to
understand at the end of the trick that they have somehow changed places.

Position the two notes as shown in the first illustration. They should
form a "V" pointing towards you, but the top note should be clear of the edges
of the note below, especially at the bottom where they are closest to you.

Start to roll the notes up, rolling both together. Keep it as neat as you can, and
continue rolling the notes until you get to the end of the bottom note. At this
point, there will still be some of the top note left to roll up. As you roll on, the
tip of the note that was on the bottom will flip over the roll. Put a finger on it,
without making it obvious that you are doing so, stop rolling, and start to unroll
the notes again. You can release your finger once you have started to carefully
unroll the notes toward you.

When you finish unrolling the notes, the one that was on the bottom—in the
illustrations here, it is the brown note—will now be on top!

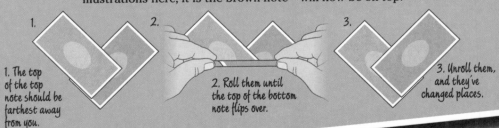

1. The top
of the top
note should be
farthest away
from you.

2. Roll them until
the top of the bottom
note flips over.

3. Unroll them,
and they've
changed places.

63 PIN THE TAIL ON THE DONKEY

2+ PLAYERS

Nothing seems easier than finding the donkey's rear end to restore its tail, but you'll be amazed at where that poor donkey's tail ends up!

What you will need:

• A blindfold • A large sheet of paper that can be hung on a wall (a leftover piece of wallpaper is ideal) • A strip of paper to represent the donkey's tail • A marker • A ruler

What you must do:

Mark the basic outline of a donkey on the paper, making it as big as possible, but don't give it a tail.

Each player then takes a turn being blindfolded and attempting to place the donkey's tail in the right position. They start from the same point right in front of the donkey, three or four steps back from the wall. Before they set off, they gently turn around three times. Make sure there are others on each side to stop the player from wandering off in totally the wrong direction.

The player then has to hold the tail against the illustration where he or she thinks it should go. Actually pinning the tail to the wall is not necessary. The blindfold is removed, and a mark is made on the illustration with the player's initials beside it.

The closest to the pre-marked tail site—the ruler can be used to decide—is the winner.

64

THE CLIMBING RING

You can make people believe that an
ordinary ring can defy gravity!

What you will need:

• A rubber band (the longer the better) • A ring

What you must do:

Tell your audience that you can make the ring defy gravity by climbing up
a rubber band. Show them the rubber band and the ring—you can even
borrow the ring from a willing volunteer if you like.

Hold the rubber band in one hand, with a small portion of the band sticking
up between your thumb and forefinger. Put the ring over this section of
rubber band, and pull the band tight between your hands, with your pulling
hand slightly higher. Make sure that you grip the rubber band really
tightly in your lower hand. You have to keep the larger portion of the
rubber band hidden behind the fingers of this hand.

When you stretch the small portion of the band, you should keep the ring
resting on the thumb and forefinger of your lower hand. Now you are
ready to make the ring climb up the rubber band.

In fact, the ring will not move up the band at all but will cling to the
same spot. It will look like it is climbing because you will slowly be
easing your grip with your lower hand. This allows more rubber to slip out
between your thumb and forefinger and relaxes the tension on the band.

You must keep your hands the same distance apart and your upper hand
the same height above the lower. The more of the rubber band you are able
to release from your lower hand, the farther the ring will appear to
climb toward your upper hand.

The ring can never make it all the way up, since it will stop when you run out of rubber band in your lower hand and the tension has all gone. That's when you call a halt to the trick with the usual magician's flourish and return the ring with thanks to your kind volunteer.

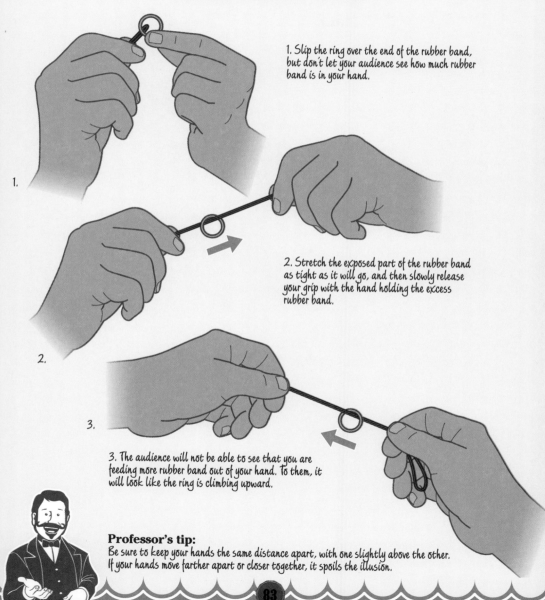

1.

1. Slip the ring over the end of the rubber band, but don't let your audience see how much rubber band is in your hand.

2.

2. Stretch the exposed part of the rubber band as tight as it will go, and then slowly release your grip with the hand holding the excess rubber band.

3.

3. The audience will not be able to see that you are feeding more rubber band out of your hand. To them, it will look like the ring is climbing upward.

Professor's tip:
Be sure to keep your hands the same distance apart, with one slightly above the other. If your hands move farther apart or closer together, it spoils the illusion.

2+ PLAYERS

FLYING PENCIL

You will struggle to keep control of this amazing pencil as it soars toward the ceiling!

What you will need:

• A pencil

What you must do:

Lay the pencil on the table, pick it up, wave it around, and talk about how, with a little concentration, you can make it rise toward the ceiling.

Grip the pencil in a closed fist with the back of your hand facing upward. Use the magic word "Ascendium," and let your hand drift higher as though the pencil is pushing it up. Grip your wrist with your free hand to stop it from going any higher.

At this point, you can open your fingers and say to everyone, "Look—I'm not holding on to it. It's pushing my hand upward!" and it will look like the pencil is, indeed, pushing against your hand.

What you have actually done, without anyone being able to see, is to extend the forefinger of the hand that is gripping your wrist and use it to hold the pencil in place.

Use the magic word "Descendium," and slowly lower the pencil back down toward the table, releasing your forefinger when it is near the tabletop and letting your wrist go.

1. Use one hand to try to hold down your rising wrist.

2. Secretly hold on to the pencil.

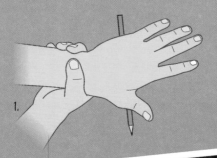
1.

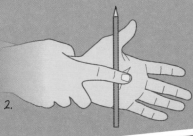
2.

66 MIND READING

Amaze your friends with your
ability to read minds!

What you will need:

• An accomplice

What you must do:

Secretly plan this trick in advance with an accomplice. No one must
know you are working together. Gather your friends around a table,
and tell them that you can read minds. Place an object in the middle
of the table—a book would do—then leave the room.

Someone in the room must pick up the book, and it will be your job
to say who it was by reading their minds. When you come back into
the room, pick up the book, concentrate, then announce who
it was that touched it.

How did you know? Your accomplice told you. You need to plan a
code with your accomplice. When you come back into the room,
your accomplice should be sitting with his or her hands on the table
or with their arms folded. If their hands are on the table with two
fingers of the right hand extended, it means that the person sitting
two places to the right was the one who touched the book. You can
use the same signal technique with the left hand, or with the arms
folded, where the hand showing on the left or right
displays the finger code.

As long as no one sees you checking the code,
you will look like a mind reader!

Bottle up

Balance a bottle upside down on top of a banknote, and challenge your friends to take the note without touching or tipping the bottle.

What you will need:

• A banknote • An empty bottle (a glass bottle works best since it is heavier)

What you must do:

Lay the banknote flat on a table and stand the bottle on top of it, balanced on its open end. The challenge is to get the banknote out from under the bottle without tipping it over.

The temptation for most people is to try to whip the note out quickly, like when you sometimes see a stage magician whipping a tablecloth out from beneath dishes laid on the table. That is very unlikely ever to work.

What you have to do is to treat the banknote and the bottle very gently. Roll the banknote from one edge until it reaches the bottle, then roll it even more carefully as it nestles up against the bottle.

Rolling the note will push the bottle at the same time as dragging the rest of the note out from underneath. If you are very careful, you can get the whole banknote out without toppling the bottle.

Roll the note gently and smoothly, keeping a constant pressure on the bottle once you reach it.

ART GALLERY

4+
PLAYERS

Use your imagination and creativity to
turn yourself into a gallery guide.

What you will need:

• Pencils and paper for everyone • A watch or clock

What you must do:

This game involves a whole range of skills, fun, and playacting,
but you don't have to be an expert in any area to join in and
have lots of laughs.

There are no winners or losers in this game—the emphasis is
on having fun. Everyone is given a sheet of paper and a pencil.
You must then draw the silliest thing you can. Anything that
comes into your head will do—a weird shape, a strange face,
a building, or simply an abstract pattern.

After ten minutes or so, everyone puts their drawings in the
middle of the table, and each player has to pick one at random.
The players then have two minutes to study the drawing.

Everyone then takes turns acting like an art gallery guide,
describing exactly what is in the drawing, inventing some
history behind the artwork, or explaining what was going
through the artist's mind when he or she created it.

The sillier the drawings are, the more entertaining the
gallery guides' explanations will be!

69

THE FORTUNE-TELLER

Use this paper gadget to predict people's fortunes.

What you will need:

• A square sheet of paper about 8.5 inches square • A pencil

What you must do:

First, you must make your basic Fortune-Teller. Fold the paper in half diagonally to create a triangle. Unfold and then fold it in half again in the opposite direction. Your square should now have fold marks dividing it into four triangles.

Fold one corner into the center spot, and crease the fold by rubbing your thumbnail along it to hold it in place. Fold the other three corners into the center as well.

Now turn the paper over, and fold each corner of your new square into the center. You should be left with eight triangles facing you. Using the pencil, number these triangles from 1 to 8. Then lift up the flaps, and beneath each number write a different "fortune"—a short phrase such as "You will find great riches in foreign lands" or "You will become a great leader."

Once you have written eight "fortunes," close all the flaps and fold your Fortune-Teller in half. You will now have four pockets on the outside, two facing you and two behind. Slip your thumbs and forefingers into the pocket, and push them out to form a tentlike structure.

You should now be able to push your fingers apart forward to open the "mouth" of the Fortune-Teller, pull them back to the middle to close it, and then pull them out to the sides to open it in the other direction. You will be able to see different numbers inside when you open it forward from those you see when you open it sideways.

Once you have the Fortune-Teller working, you can flatten it and draw pictures of animals on the outside of the finger pockets. The animals will be the first choice that you give when you are telling someone's fortune. If you have, for example, drawn an elephant, a penguin, a giraffe, and a monkey, you must ask your subject to choose which of the animals they like best. If the elephant is chosen, you then work your Fortune-Teller open and closed, calling out one letter for each move: E–L–E–P–H–A–N–T.

You then hold the Fortune-Teller open on the final move, and ask your subject to choose a number from those in view. If 4 is in view and is chosen, you work the Fortune-Teller open and closed four times and ask your subject to choose another number.

This is where the subject's fortune is actually told because now you flatten the Fortune-Teller on the table, opening it up with all of the numbers showing. You lift the flap marked with the chosen number and read what is written under the flap.

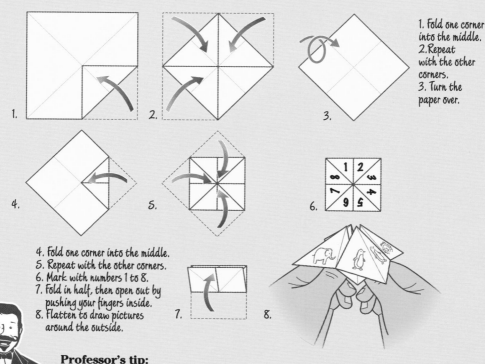

1. Fold one corner into the middle.
2. Repeat with the other corners.
3. Turn the paper over.

1.

2.

3.

4.

5.

6.

4. Fold one corner into the middle.
5. Repeat with the other corners.
6. Mark with numbers 1 to 8.
7. Fold in half, then open out by pushing your fingers inside.
8. Flatten to draw pictures around the outside.

7.

8.

Professor's tip:
Create a new Fortune-Teller with different fortunes once all of the old fortunes have been told.

FLOATING PENCIL

Make a pencil move up and down inside an empty bottle.

What you will need:

• A bottle (preferably with dark glass) • A pencil • A piece of thread

What you must do:

This is another trick that you must prepare in advance and be able to set up quickly, simply by turning your back to the audience, making it look like you are picking the bottle up from a table behind you.

Hold the bottle in your left hand in front of you, and use your right hand to make lots of conjuring moves, waving it around the bottle to tempt the pencil out. The pencil will rise and start to climb out of the top of the bottle, then sink back down again on your command.

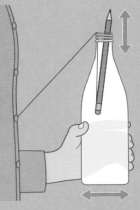

What the audience can't see is that there is a thread tied around the bottom of the pencil. In the illustration shown here, the bottle is clear and the thread is obvious, but with a darker bottle, especially if you are wearing a dark shirt, the thread will be very difficult to see. The illustration shows a side view of how the trick works. Your audience will see it with you facing them, again making the thread hard to see.

The other end of the thread needs to be wound around a button on the front of your shirt, or your belt buckle, whichever is easiest for you to do quickly with your back to the audience when you first pick up the bottle. Then you can make the pencil rise by pushing your left hand away from your body, and make it fall to the bottom again by bringing your hand closer to your body.

From the side, it is clear how the trick works, but from the front, where the audience is, it is a mystery.

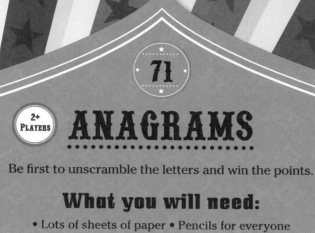

2+ PLAYERS — ANAGRAMS

Be first to unscramble the letters and win the points.

What you will need:

• Lots of sheets of paper • Pencils for everyone

What you must do:

One player must act as the judge, and everyone takes a turn being the judge.

Each player is given a piece of paper and a pencil. The judge calls out a topic. It might be "Animals" or "Cities." Everyone must then write down the name of an animal or a city, using big letters but being careful that no one else sees.

They then figure out an anagram of that name—a word or phrase that uses the same letters. "Horse" could become "shore" or "Rome" could become "more." Keep your figuring out on the same side of the paper, then turn the paper over to write your new word or phrase on the back.

One by one, each person holds up their anagram for everyone to see and the first person to call out the original word gets a point. The judge can join in calling out the solutions but does not write down an anagram.

The person sitting to the right of the judge now takes on the judge's role and thinks of a new topic.

Treasure Hunt

Find the clues that lead to the treasure horde.

What you will need:

• Ten pieces of paper • A pencil • A big bag of wrapped candy

What you must do:

This is an ideal game for parents or older kids to set up for younger children and requires a little preparation. The first thing to do is to choose a hiding place for your treasure horde of candy.

Next, write out ten clues and hide them around the house, in the yard, or anywhere to which the treasure hunters will have easy access. If there are lots of treasure hunters, split them into teams, but make it clear from the outset that there is a treasure chest—a bowl or a large plate sitting on a table, to which all of the treasure must be brought to be divided fairly between everyone at the end of the game.

Now you give or read out a clue and send your treasure hunters off to try and figure it out. The clue could be something like, "New York's nickname will lead you to the next clue." They will remember New York's "Big Apple" nickname, and rush to the kitchen where they will find the next clue along with the apples in the fruit bowl— and a couple of candy pieces to keep them interested.

The clues eventually lead to the big bag of candy that can then be shared. You can do more than ten clues, but the more clues there are, the longer the treasure hunt will take.

Professor's tip:
Try to keep the clues lighthearted, and be on hand to give hints to younger children if they are struggling to figure them out.

FISHING FOR ICE CUBES

2+
PLAYERS

How can you use a thread to fish an ice cube out of a glass of water without touching the glass, the water, or the ice cube?

What you will need:

• A glass • Some cold water • An ice cube • A thread • Some salt

What you must do:

First, you have to drop an ice cube—preferably a fresh ice cube straight from the freezer—into a glass of cold water. Now you can challenge everyone to try to get the ice cube out of the glass using a strand of thread and without touching the ice, the water, or the glass.

Seems impossible? You can't tie a thread around an ice cube without touching the water, after all, can you? In fact, you don't need to.

The trick is simply to lay the thread across the top of the ice cube and then sprinkle a little salt over the ice. The salt will dissolve the surface of the ice cube, but it will refreeze almost right away, and the thread will be frozen to the surface.

You can then lift the ice cube out of the water, dangling from the end of the thread that is frozen to it.

Pouring a little salt on the ice cube will melt its surface momentarily.

Make sure that you do not allow the salted ice cube to touch your skin, and allow the cube to dissolve in the glass before pouring the water away.

74

THE SECRET COIN

2+
PLAYERS

Make a coin vanish from the palm of your hand.

What you will need:

• Four coins • Some silver foil the same shade as the coins • Scissors

What you must do:

Preparation and practice, as always with conjuring tricks, are essential to make it look like a coin in your hand has simply vanished.

The preparation involves making a fake coin. Cover one side and the edges of one of the coins with the silver foil (you can use other colors of foil for different types of coin), and press the foil against the coin, rubbing it with your thumb.

The foil will take on an impression of the coin. You must then carefully remove it from the coin, so that it retains its shape. Trim off any excess foil, but make sure to leave the foil that was around the rim of the coin, so that your fake coin will look like it is as thick as a normal coin.

With your fake coin prepared, you are ready to go in front of your audience. Show the audience four coins in your hand. It's best if the three real ones can conceal the fake coin a little.

You can then clap your hands closed, rub them together, and make a big show of telling your audience that simply by rubbing your hands together, you can make one of the coins vanish.

What you will actually be doing is scrunching up your fake coin. With a little practice, you should be able to roll it into a

ball small enough to hide between your fingers when
you open your hands again.

As far as your audience is concerned, one of the coins
will simply have disappeared.

1. The foil that you use should be
a little bigger than the coin and
roughly the same shade.

1.

2.

2. Gently rub the foil until it
takes on the impression of the
coin, then fold the foil down
around the edges to give your
fake coin some depth.

3. With the excess foil neatly trimmed
off, display it in your hand slightly
hidden by the other coins.

3.

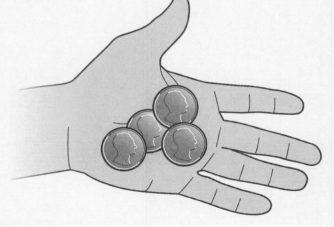

Professor's tip:
You need to be able to hide the scrunched-up fake coin effectively, and to do that, you will
have to put in a little practice before you try this trick on an audience.

CHEAT

In this card game, the biggest cheat is usually the winner.

What you will need:

• A deck of cards (two decks if there are more than four players)

What you must do:

The dealer deals out all of the cards. The players look at their cards, and the player to the dealer's left goes first. He or she places up to four cards face down in the middle of the table to start a discard pile.

Players have to announce what they are placing down, and their discards must be sets. They can have a "run" of four of the same suit—the four, five, six and seven of spades, for example. They can also have four of a kind—four threes, four nines, or four kings, perhaps.

No one sees what is being discarded, but if a player says they are discarding four fives and you have three fives in your hand, they are obviously cheating (although it's not so easy to tell when you are playing with two decks) and you yell "Cheat!"

The last cards to be discarded are then turned over. If the player who played them was cheating, that player has to take all of the cards from the discard pile. If the player who called "Cheat!" was wrong, that player has to take all of the cards.

The first person to get rid of all of their cards is the winner.

FIFTEENS

This game takes more concentration
and strategy than it might seem.

What you will need:

• Fifteen toothpicks

What you must do:

This simple game is said to have originated in ancient China and is
a more advanced form of Pick-Up Sticks (see p26). It involves fifteen
toothpicks (or you can use coins or playing cards) arranged in a
particular way.

The toothpicks are in seven rows. There is one in the first row.
Beneath that, there are two in the second row. Beneath that, there
are three in the third row, then two more rows of three, a row of
two, and a final, single toothpick.

You and your opponent must take turns picking up toothpicks.
You can pick up one from a row, or two, or the complete row,
but you can only take from one row at a time.

The last one to pick up a toothpick is the winner.

THE TOOTHPICK TRICK

2+ PLAYERS

Make a toothpick vanish from your hand
before your audience's eyes.

What you will need:

• An ordinary toothpick • A finger ring

What you must do:

Practice over and over again! This sleight-of-hand party trick looks good
when you get it right, but you need to have nimble, well-trained fingers to
be able to do it quickly and smoothly enough to fool your audience.

Tell your audience that you can make the toothpick vanish, and explain
that it is a mysterious magic skill that has been passed down through
the centuries by wise men and magicians. You will have to practice your
speech as much as you will your finger movements to make this trick as
entertaining as possible.

Keep your hands on the move all the time that you are talking. At first,
you can show your audience the toothpick held between your thumb and
forefinger, but you must keep your hands moving, passing your free hand
in front of the one holding the toothpick again and again, so that no one
will be able to see what you are up to.

What you will be doing is slipping the toothpick between your fingers and
pushing it through your finger ring. The ring will hold it securely behind
your hand. When you open your hand, you show the audience only your
empty palm, keeping the back of your hand facing away from them.

At first, this is an awkward thing to try to do quickly, so when you are
practicing, start off by doing it slowly. Before too long, you will be able
to slip the toothpick between your fingers and through the ring
in the blink of an eye.

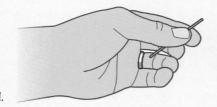

1. You need to be wearing a ring for this trick, and you start by holding the toothpick so that the audience can see it clearly.

1.

2. While mvoing your hand around and talking to distract the audience, quickly tuck the toothpick between your fingers.

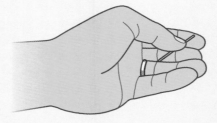

2.

3. The audience will not see you slipping the toothpick between your ring and the back of your finger, where it can be hidden.

3.

4. With a final flourish, show your open hand with the toothpick having apparently disappeared into thin air.

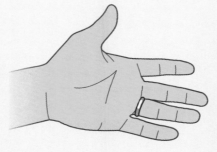

4.

Professor's tip:
Keeping both hands on the move and talking to your audience will distract them, but you do need to practice hiding the toothpick swiftly.

2+
PLAYERS

STANDING TUBE

This trick looks impossible, even when you see it working before your very eyes!

What you will need:

• A cardboard tube from inside a toilet-paper roll

What you must do:

Challenge your friends to drop the tube onto a table, so that it stands up vertically, balanced on one end.

Most people will drop the tube so that it hits the table end first, thinking that that is the best way to finish with a standing cardboard column, but the tube will bounce and fall over.

The way to make it stand on end is actually to drop it so that it lands on its side. It will then bounce up and stand on one end. You will have to practice a little to find the right height from which to drop it. Somewhere around 6 inches tends to work.

It may not bounce and stand up every time, but you can expect it to work at least once in every three drops.

Professor's tip:
If this trick doesn't work for you the first time, keep trying, but also try dropping the tube with a little force to make sure that it bounces.

LIMERICK TAG

2+ PLAYERS

Take turns making up a silly limerick, one line at a time.

What you will need:

• A watch or clock

What you must do:

Everyone has to make up a line of a limerick to add to the line that has gone before. If there are lots of you, you can split into teams to work together on your lines.

A limerick is a poem with five lines, and it always scans the same way, such as:

A girl soaked her father with water
From a squirter that he had bought her
She laughed like mad
Until she saw Dad
Had a squirter for soaking his daughter!

One player or team is chosen to start, and the next player has 30 seconds to come up with the next line. You can make the rhyme as silly as you like, but if you can't come up with something, you are out of that round and have a penalty point marked against you. The others continue playing.

The player who finishes the limerick then has to start a new one, and the player or team at the end of the limerick session with the fewest penalty points is the winner.

TUMBLING EGGS

The challenge is to flip an egg
without actually touching it at all.

What you will need:

• A raw egg • A shot glass (small glass used for liquor)

What you must do:

Put the egg in the shot glass, with the wider end of the egg sitting inside
the glass. Your challenge is to turn the egg upside down without
touching the egg or the glass.

The way to do it is to lean over the egg, so that you are directly over the
very top of the shell, and then blow down on the egg. Try it gently at first,
but when you blow with just the right strength, the egg will
miraculously jump up in the air and turn over.

To impress your audience, you can then crack the egg into a bowl or a
larger glass to show them that you weren't using any type of a trick egg.

Lean over the egg so
that you can blow down
directly onto the point,
to make the egg do
a somersault.

DOWSING FOR CARDS

Astound your audience by using a pencil to dowse for a hidden card.

What you will need:

• A deck of cards • A pencil or pen

What you must do:

Fan out the deck of cards in your hands, and offer it to a volunteer, asking him or her to pick a card. Hold the fanned deck face down so that you can't see the cards and tell your volunteer not to show you the chosen card.

Close the fanned deck, and as you do so, sneak a look at the card on the bottom. Let's say it's the three of hearts. Put the deck face down on the table, and ask your volunteer to put the chosen card face down on top. Ask the volunteer to cut the deck, putting the bottom half on top of the top half.

The chosen card now looks like it is buried in the deck, but you know that the bottom card in the deck was the three of hearts. You also know that it is now sitting on top of the chosen card.

Take the deck and spread the cards out face up in a long line, so that you can see part of each one. Now wave your pencil over the cards, and when you get to the three of hearts, make it start to wobble up and down. You say, "I think we've got something here!" then let the end of the pencil drop onto the card next to the three of hearts, the one that was below it, which you now know is the card that your volunteer chose.

2 PLAYERS

TIP-TAP HANDS

Challenge your opponent to see who has the quickest hands and the fastest reflexes!

What you will need:

- All you need is to be wide awake and concentrating hard.

What you must do:

Put your hands together, palm to palm, with your fingers pointing straight out in front of you. Now stand in front of your opponent, each of you pointing your hands toward the other.

You should both be holding your hands out in front with your elbows touching your stomach and your forearms parallel with the ground. Now you must move close, so that the tips of your fingers are touching the tips of your opponent's fingers.

Decide who will go first. If it is you, what you must do is move either your left or right hand and tap the back of your opponent's hand. Your opponent has to move his or her hands, still pressed together, out of the way as fast as possible but must not move at all until you move. If you fake a move in order to make your opponent move, you lose your turn.

You score one point for a tap or if your opponent moves before you do. If you make a tap, you get to go again. If your opponent gets out of the way in time and you miss a tap, it is then your opponent's turn to go for a tap. The first one to score 25 points is the winner.

Professor's tip:
You have to be quick when you make a move, but take as long as you like to do so. That way, your opponent may panic and move, giving you the point.

CONSEQUENCES

2+ PLAYERS

Take turns writing a line of a story that
will have a surprise ending.

What you will need:

• A sheet of paper for each player • A pencil for each player

What you must do:

Each player writes an adjective at the top of his or her sheet, describing a man. It
could say "Happy" or you can write more, such as "Very angry, wearing pink socks."

The first line is folded over and the sheet passed to the left, so that everyone has a
different sheet to add the next line at the top of the page. The next line must be a
man's name. It can be someone you all know or a completely made-up name. The
paper is then folded over and passed on once more for the next new line to be added.

The sequence of lines goes as follows:

1. Adjective or phrase describing a man
2. A man's name
3. The word MET followed by an adjective or phrase describing a woman
4. A woman's name
5. The word AT followed by the place where they met
6. The words HE SAID followed by what he said
7. The words SHE SAID followed by what she said
8. The words THE CONSEQUENCE WAS followed by what happened
9. The words THE WORLD THOUGHT followed by what everyone thought about it

Once everyone has written what the world thought about the meeting, pass the papers
on one more time, open them up, and take turns reading out the ridiculous stories!

BINGO

2+ PLAYERS

Be the first to check off all your numbers and shout "BINGO!"

What you will need:

• Paper for each player • Paper for making numbers
• Pencils for each player • Scissors • A bag or hat

What you must do:

Each player draws a grid five boxes wide by five boxes deep. Players then mark five numbers in each of the five columns, leaving only the box in the center of the grid blank. The numbers must be marked in a specific way.

In the first column, you have only numbers from 1 to 15. In the second column, you have only numbers from 16 to 30. In the third column, you have only numbers from 31 to 45, with the third box down left blank as it is the center box. This box is a "free" space that does not have to be filled. The fourth column has numbers between 46 and 60, while the fifth has numbers between 61 and 75. No number can be used more than once.

A "caller" must be chosen, and this player draws another grid ten squares by eight squares. In each box the caller writes one number, going from 1 to 75, leaving five unused boxes. This grid must then be cut into lots of little numbered squares. The five blanks are discarded.

The caller puts all of these numbers into the bag or hat, and the game begins. The caller takes one number from the hat and calls it out. If you have that number on your grid, you cross it off. The caller then takes another number from the hat, and play continues in this way until one player has crossed off all of their numbers in a vertical, horizontal or diagonal row. That player calls out "BINGO!" and is the minor winner. Play then continues until someone has crossed out all of their numbers and calls out "BINGO!" That player is the grand champion.

CROSSWORDS

Be the first one to finish your crossword
puzzle with the most words.

What you will need:

• Paper for each player • Pencils for each player

What you must do:

Each player draws a grid on their paper, six boxes wide by six boxes
deep—you can make the grids bigger if you want the game to last longer.

Players then take turns calling out a letter of the alphabet, and everyone
must mark that letter somewhere on their grid.

The aim is to create words running horizontally or vertically on the grid.
Words on one line or running directly above or below each other must
be separated by shaded squares, so that they don't touch, but vertical
words can intersect horizontal words.

Think carefully where you put the letters that are called out, so that you
can construct words, leaving spaces while you wait for the letters that
you need to be called. Letters can be called more than once.

When you have filled up your grid, you drop out of the
game and do not call letters. When there is just one
person left calling, the game is over, and the one with
the most words on their grid is the winner.

WISH YOU WERE HERE

Take a stroll through your favorite vacation spot.

What you will need:

• A vacation postcard • A pair of scissors

What you must do:

"Wish you were here" is what people used to write on postcards that they sent home when they were on vacation to let their friends and family know how much they were missing them.

You can use those words as part of your presentation to the audience when you set yourself the challenge of walking through the vacation scene shown on the postcard, or if it's a stunning view of the sparkling sea by a sunny beach, tell them you are going to dive in head first!

Then, take the postcard and fold it in half lengthwise. Use the scissors to make a series of cuts from the fold out toward the edge of the postcard. Make the cuts about half an inch apart but do not cut all the way to the edge.

Next, make a series of cuts from the edge in toward the fold. These cuts need to be between the first set of cuts, and they must not go all the way to the fold.

Now open the postcard flat and cut along the fold, but do not cut from the edge. Start from the first cut that you made, and carefully work your way along to the last of the first set of cuts.

Gently pull the edges of the card, and you will find that you have created a continuous zigzag strip of card that you will be able to step through or even pull down over your head, so that you are diving head first into the sea!

1.

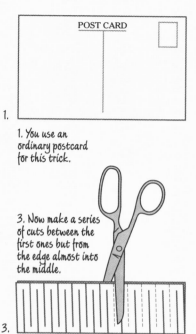

1. You use an ordinary postcard for this trick.

2.

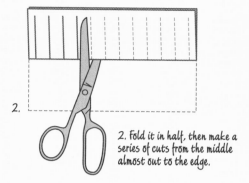

2. Fold it in half, then make a series of cuts from the middle almost out to the edge.

3. Now make a series of cuts between the first ones but from the edge almost into the middle.

3.

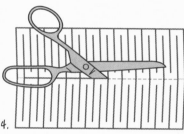

4.

4. Open the card out and cut down the middle but not right from the edge, and stop short of the other edge.

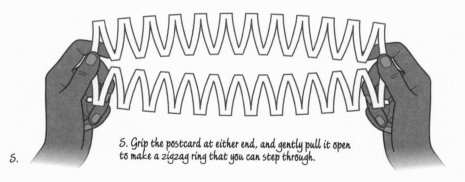

5.

5. Grip the postcard at either end, and gently pull it open to make a zigzag ring that you can step through.

Professor's tip:
Try to stop your cuts the same distance from the edge each time, in order to give you a strong, even strip when you open it all out.

SNAKE TRAP

The snake has poisonous fangs and mustn't
be allowed to bite itself!

What you will need:

• Paper and a pencil

What you must do:

Mark a grid of dots on the paper ten dots wide by ten dots deep. The dots
should be about half an inch apart. The first player then draws a line connecting
two dots. The line can be vertical or horizontal but not diagonal. The second
player adds another line connecting one end of the first line to an adjacent dot.
The line can go across, or up, or down, but not diagonally.

You can add lines to either end of the snake, and it can go anywhere on the grid,
but neither end of the snake is allowed to touch its body. This, you see, is a
highly poisonous snake with a head at either end—and if it bites itself, it dies.

The players must try to draw their lines in such a way that they force
their opponent to be the one who must eventually draw the line
that turns the snake on itself.

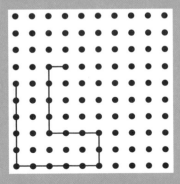

BLOW FOOTBALL

The player or team with the most hot air wins!

What you will need:

• A drinking straw for each player • A ping-pong ball (or scrunched-up paper ball) • Books, mugs, or other items to act as goalposts

What you must do:

Set up your goals at either end of a table or on the floor. Each player then chooses a position around the table or around the floor space chosen as a "field." Players must not move from their positions, although they can lean and stretch as much as they like. The ball is placed in the center of the table, and the game begins when someone shouts "Blow!" The two players closest to the ball must then blow through their straws to send the ball toward the opponent's goal.

As the ball comes within range, other players join in to blow the ball away from their goal or toward the other goal.

The winners are the players who have scored the most goals by the time everyone has run out of breath!

IT'S IN THE CARDS

Read the mind of your willing volunteer to find the mystery card.

2+ PLAYERS

What you will need:

• A deck of cards that you don't mind marking

What you must do:

Prepare this trick secretly beforehand. Shuffle the cards and split the deck in half. On the backs of one half, write random numbers between 1 and 52 but with no eights. On the backs of the other half, write the number 8 on every one. Put the two halves together with the cards marked 8 on the bottom.

Show a volunteer a fan spread of the cards. Be sure to fan out only those cards from the bottom of the deck, the ones that are all marked 8 on the back. Do not let anyone see the backs of the cards. Ask the volunteer to choose a card mentally, without touching it, and to concentrate on it because you are going to read his or her mind.

Close up the cards, covering the deck with your hands so no one can see the number. Look like you are concentrating, then say, "Your card was an eight." That's unlikely to be true, but if it is, then you have already performed a trick—good going! It is more likely that they will say no.

Deal a few cards from the top of the deck face down to show that they have numbers on the back. Say, "I am getting a strong sense that it was an eight. I have numbered these cards so that I always know they are in a random order. None of these is yours."

Look like you are giving up. Turn the cards in your hand over, and fan them out. Ask the volunteer to pick out the hidden card. Since it has come from what was the bottom half of the deck, you can take the card, turn it over and say, "Ah, this is what was confusing me …" because on the back is written the number 8.

Professor's tip:
Don't let anyone see that ALL of the cards from that part of the deck have 8 on the back. Put the cards away before they can be examined.

RHYME TIME

2+
PLAYERS

Play a guessing game where you find
the missing word through rhyme.

What you will need:

• Paper and pencils for each player

What you must do:

Decide who will go first. That player must then
think of a word, write it down, but not let anyone see it.

The player then gives a clue by saying, "I know a word that
rhymes with …" and give a rhyming word. If the mystery
word that the player wrote down was, for example, "head,"
the player could say, "I know a word that rhymes with red."

Each player then takes turns asking a question, without
mentioning the word they think might be the mystery word.

A player might ask, "Is it somewhere you might sleep?"
The first player would then say, "No, it's not 'bed'."

Play then continues until someone asks a question to
which the answer is yes, such as, "Is it a part of your body?"
The first player will answer yes and the questioner can
then say, "Is it head?" The first player must then show the
word on the paper to confirm that the guess is correct.

The player who guesses correctly then starts the game again
by writing down a new word and giving a new rhyming clue.

ACROSTICS

Guess the word by figuring out the clues.

What you will need:

• Pencil and paper for each player

What you must do:

Decide on a topic. Each person must then think of a word concerned with that topic. If the topic is buildings, the word might be "office" or "palace."

Write down your word, but keep it to yourself. Then think of clues for other words that start with each of the letters of your chosen word.

Palace might work like this:

He catches criminals	**P**oliceman
It's not before, it's	**A**fter
A giggle that exploded	**L**augh
Small crawling insect	**A**nt
A vehicle with wheels	**C**ar
It contains only one letter	**E**nvelope

Each player takes a turn giving a clue, and the others must write down the letter to which they think the clue points.

When it is your turn to give a clue, you can also try to guess one other player's word. You get a point for each one you guess correctly, and the player with the most points at the end of your acrostic session is the winner.

2+
PLAYERS

NUMBER MAGIC

Find a number someone has thought
of, and then tell them their age.

What you will need:

Pencils and paper for everyone and a calculator if required

What you must do:

Ask everyone to think of a five-digit number. Then double it.
Then add 5. Then multiply it by 50. Then add their age.
Then add the number of days in the year (365). Finally, subtract 615.

The answer will be a seven-figure number. The first five numbers will
be the number first thought of, and the last two will be the player's age.

Let's say you thought of the number	21,485
Double it	42,970
Add 5	42,975
Multiply by 50	2,148,750
Add your age (we'll say you're 12)	2,148,762
Add 365	2,149,127
Subtract 615	2,148,512

Ask each player to show you their answers, and you will
be able to tell them the number they first thought of and
their age—providing they added up correctly!

SECRET FOURS

Collect the most sets of four to win.

4+
PLAYERS

What you will need:

• A deck of cards

What you must do:

Each player is dealt five cards, and the rest are put in a stack in the middle of the table. They study their cards, then the player to the left of the dealer begins.

The first player asks any other player for specific cards. If, for instance, you had two tens in your hand, you would ask the other player, "Do you have any tens?" You must have at least one ten in your hand to ask for tens. If the player has any tens, they have to hand them over.

The first player can then continue by asking any other player either for tens or any other card. When he is refused, he picks up a card from the stack, and play passes to the next player.

The object is to collect cards of the same rank, four sevens, four tens, or four queens. When you have a set, you place it face up on the table in front of you. The player who collects the most sets by the time all of the cards are used up is the winner.

Professor's tip:
Remember what other players ask for, so that you know what they are collecting, then ask them for the same thing if you can.

TABOO

2+ PLAYERS

Answer The Inquisitor's questions without using the forbidden word.

What you will need:

• Paper • A pencil

What you must do:

One of the players is chosen as The Inquisitor. The Inquisitor declares a certain word or words to be taboo. Start off with just one or two taboo words, but make them frequently used words like "the" or "and."

Taboo words must not be used when answering The Inquisitor's questions.

The Inquisitor then asks the first player a question, which can be anything, such as "What did you do on Sunday?" or "Describe the outside of your house." The player must answer without using any taboo words.

If anyone hears a taboo word being used, they have to yell "TABOO!" and the player who used the forbidden word is out of the game.

The last player left in is the winner and becomes The Inquisitor for the next round.

95

SHROUD OF MYSTERY

?+
PLAYERS

Use the Shroud of Mystery to make a
coin disappear into thin air.

What you will need:

• A cloth or napkin to serve as your
Shroud of Mystery • An ordinary coin

What you must do:

Explain to your audience that your Shroud of Mystery has magic
properties and can make a coin vanish from your hand. It is important
that, while you are talking to your audience, you move your Shroud of
Mystery around, draping it over your hand and generally making
your audience pay attention to the cloth, whether they know
that they are doing so or not.

Hold the cloth clasped between your index finger and middle finger.
This looks very casual and allows you to drape the cloth over
either hand as you move it around. The purpose of the cloth,
after all, is to conceal what you will be doing.

Pick up a coin and hold it in your other hand. Balance it on top
of your closed fist, and then show the coin in the palm of
your hand before you close your hand around it. Then hold up
your closed fist again, this time with the coin held tightly inside.

Pass the Shroud of Mystery over your closed fist a couple of
times and tell the audience that you can still feel the coin in your
hand until, with one final flourish, you run the cloth over your hand,
dragging it from behind your fist, over the top, and down in front. The
instant that the cloth is hiding your fist from the audience, let the coin
drop from your fist into the open palm of your other hand.

At that point, you can announce that you no longer feel the coin in your hand, open your fist, and show everyone that the Shroud of Mystery has made the coin disappear.

1. Show your audience the coin, then hold it in your closed fist. Hold the cloth as shown, so that you can waft it over your closed hand.

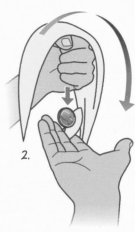

2. Pass the cloth over your hand a few times while talking to the audience, then on a final pass, drop the coin from one hand into the other.

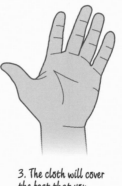

3. The cloth will cover the fact that you opened your hand and dropped the coin, so you can now show everyone that the coin has vanished.

Professor's tip:
You need to use the Shroud of Mystery to cover what you are doing with your hands, and as in all magic tricks, practice makes perfect.

2+
PLAYERS

REVERSE CARD

The hidden card magically reveals
itself by turning over in the deck.

What you will need:

• A deck of cards

What you must do:

Prepare the deck of cards by holding it face down, then take the bottom
card and turn it over so that it is face up. Return it to the bottom
of the deck. The bottom card is now face up, but no one can see it.
You are now ready to face your audience.

Hold the cards spread out in a fan, face down, with the bottom (face up)
card hidden at the end of the fan. Ask your volunteer to choose
a card from the fan but not to show it to you.

While the volunteer studies the chosen card, close the fan into a deck, and
while distracting attention by talking, turn the deck over so that the
bottom card is now on top. This card will now be face down while all the
others are face up, although no one can see them in the closed deck.

Have the volunteer hide the chosen card by slipping it into the deck
somewhere in the middle. The volunteer will be putting the card in face
down, among a deck that is now secretly face up.

Put your hands behind your back, say a magic word, and flip the top
card while no one can see you doing it. You can now fan the cards out
again, holding the pack face down, and the chosen card will appear
somewhere near the middle of the fan, face up!

3+ PLAYERS

IT BEGINS WITH ...

Think of as many names as you
can beginning with the key letter.

What you will need:

• A newspaper or magazine • Pencils and paper
for everyone • A watch or clock

What you must do:

One of the players acts as the judge. The judge keeps the score,
selects the topic, and chooses the key letter.

You can decide together on a list of topics, such as singers,
movie stars, football players, artists, presidents, animals, foods …
you can make the list as long as you like.The judge chooses a topic from
the list, then waves his or her pencil over a newspaper and jabs it down
to select a random key letter.

Everyone must now think of as many names or words as they can from
the chosen topic beginning with the key letter and write them
down. For people, you can use first or second names.

After two minutes, the judge calls "Stop" and counts up
everyone's answers, awarding a point for each correct
name or word on their lists. Another player can then
become judge for the next round.

Mixed Messages

Create a silly message using the letters in a chosen word.

2+
PLAYERS

What you will need:

• A pencil and paper

What you must do:

Each player takes a turn thinking of a key word and writing it down.
The player to the left of the one who has written the word then starts the
message by saying a word that begins with the first letter of the key word.
The next player says a word beginning with the second letter, and so on.

For instance, if the key word is TELEVISION:

Player 1	**T**iny
Payer 2	**E**lephants
Player 3	**L**ike
Player 4	**E**ating
Player 5	**V**egetables
Player 6	**I**n
Player 7	**S**ocks
Player 8	**I**roned
Player 9	**O**ver
Player 10	**N**achos

Of course, you don't need ten players, you just keep taking turns until
you have used up all the letters in the word. The player who wrote the
first word has to write down each new word and then read the message.
Try to make it as silly as possible to get everyone laughing!

After reading the message, move on to the
next player's key word.

Professor's tip:
Make sure that your key words have lots of letters in them, in order to make
the message that is spelled out as silly as possible.

FIND THE COIN

Find the chosen coin using the power of your mind.

What you will need:

• Ten coins of the same value, so that they are exactly the same size
• A cloth or plastic bag • A blindfold • A marker

What you must do:

Put all of the coins into the bag, and then ask a volunteer to choose one. Your volunteer must then use the marker to write his or her initials on the coin.

When the ink is dry, ask the volunteer to hold the coin very tightly in his or her hand and to concentrate very hard on the coin. After a minute, the volunteer drops the coin into the bag, and you then shake the bag to mix them up.

The volunteer can then blindfold you and you reach into the bag to rifle through the coins. Say that you are trying to pick up the mental energy that the volunteer's concentration transferred to the coin. Then pull out the coin with the volunteer's initials on it.

How did you do it?

You felt around in the bag for the coin that was warm from being held tightly in the volunteer's hand.

MINI WORDS

Make as many small words as you can from one long word.

What you will need:

• Pencil and paper for everyone • A clock or watch

What you must do:

Players take turns coming up with a good,
long word like POLITICIAN or INVESTIGATION.

The word is written on a piece of paper, so that everyone agrees on
the spelling. Everyone then has two minutes to write down as many
small words as they can, using only the letters in the big word.

You don't have to use all of the letters in the big word, and you
can use the same letters more than once, but not more than
once in the same small word.

From POLITICIAN, for example, you could get:

CAN, TIP, CLAN, TIN, PLAN, LOT, PAN, TOIL, TO, IT, LIT, CLAP, CAP,
TAP, TAN, LIP, LAP, NIT, PIT, NAP, TOP, POT, CLOT, PIN, NIP, PICT,
PACT, PAIN, PAINT, POINT.

After two minutes, you swap sheets with the player next to you and
take turns reading out each other's answers, marking one point for
every correct word on the sheet and ten points if the player has
come up with a word that uses all of the letters from the big word.

When all the papers are marked and returned,
start again with a new big word.

101

GIN RUMMY

Collect matched sets and win points
to become the champion.

What you will need:

• A deck of cards • Pencil and paper to keep score

What you must do:

Each player is dealt ten cards. The object is to collect sets of three or four
cards. Sets can be cards of the same value or cards of the same suit running
in sequence (three, four, five and six of diamonds, for instance).

The remaining cards are placed in a stack in the middle, face down.
The top card is turned over and placed face up to start the discard pile.
The player who did not deal begins by picking up either the card off the
discard pile or one off the top of the stack. He or she must then choose
which card to discard, as you can only have ten in your hand.

If you collect a "gin hand"—say, two sets of three and a set of four—you knock
on the table to end the game as you discard your last card. You can knock
earlier, if you have a couple of good sets and some low-ranked, unmatched cards.

You get 25 points for a gin hand plus the value of your opponent's
unmatched cards. The ace counts as 1 and face cards as 10.
If you knock without a gin hand and your opponent has
a higher value of unmatched cards than you do, the
difference is the number of points you score.

Alpha Race

The clock is ticking, and you have just
60 seconds to make your list.

What you will need:

• A clock or watch • Pencil and paper for everyone
• Scissors • A dictionary

What you must do:

Write all of the letters of the alphabet on a piece of paper and
cut them out individually. Put all the letters on a table
face down and mix them up.

The first player then chooses a letter and shouts it out to
everyone. The player in charge of timing then shouts "Go!" and
everyone has one minute to write down as many words as they
can think of beginning with that letter.

After one minute, everyone must stop and pass their sheets to
the right to be checked by the player sitting next to them.
You score one point for each word.

When marking is complete, the sheets are handed back, and the
next player picks out another letter. After 26 rounds—one for
each letter of the alphabet—add up your scores and
the player with the most points wins.

To avoid arguments over whether a player's spelling is correct
or if the word exists at all, look it up in the dictionary.

THE NAME GAME

2+
PLAYERS

How would you describe yourself,
in words using your initials?

What you will need:

• A clock or watch • Pencil and paper

What you must do:

This game is all about being able to think fast, using your
imagination and letting your sense of humor shine through.

The first player has to think of a name of someone that everyone
will recognize. It could be someone in the room, a famous
personality, a family member, or a friend that everyone knows.

The next player then has 30 seconds to think of two words
to describe that person, and the words must start with
the person's initials. Professor Murphy, for example, might be
"powerful mind" or "perfect mustache."

If you come up with a description that fits or that makes
people laugh within the time limit, you score a point.

One player should be in charge of keeping the time and
another in charge of keeping everyone's scores. When you
can no longer think of any famous names, the player
with the highest score is the winner.

Professor's tip:
*Don't panic when it comes to your turn——30 seconds
is plenty of time to think of a couple of words.*

2+
PLAYERS

COMBINATION CODES

Come up with the longest word using a list of codes.

What you will need:

• Pencils and paper for everyone • A clock or watch • A dictionary

What you must do:

Pass around a piece of paper on which every player must write down a combination of two letters—AU, RT, SM, and so on. Each player writes down one combination, and the sheet ends up looking like the kind of coded message a spy might have sent.

When all the combinations have been written, the first one is called out, and everyone has one minute to think of the longest word they can that includes those letters in the order that they appear.

For AU, you could have "faulty," "Austria," "laughter," or "Australia." Each player takes turns reading out his or her word, so that everyone can agree that the word is correct. If you have not come up with a correct word, you score no points. Disputed words should be checked in the dictionary. If you have thought of a correct word, you score one point for each letter.

In the case of AU, the player who wrote "faulty" would score six, while the player who wrote "Australia" would score nine.

When you have been through all of the combination codes, add up your scores to see who has won that round, then come up with a new set of combinations to start again.